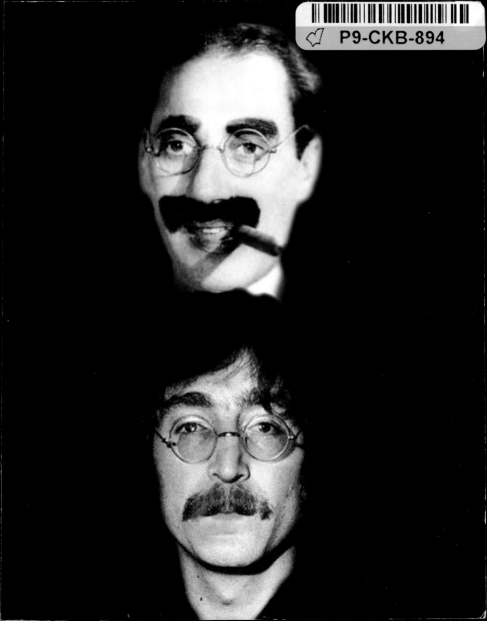

Marx & Lennon

Hellbent on Insanity

The Gilligan's Island Handbook

The Get Smart Handbook

The Partridge Family Album

Polish Your Furniture with Panty Hose

Hi Bob!

Selling Out

Paint Your House with Powdered Milk

Wash Your Hair with Whipped Cream

The Bubble Wrap Book

Joey Green's Encyclopedia of Offbeat Uses for Brand-Name Products

The Zen of Oz

The Warning Label Book

Monica Speaks

The Official Slinky Book

You Know You've Reached Middle Age If . . .

The Mad Scientist Handbook

Clean Your Clothes with Cheez Whiz

The Road to Success Is Paved with Failure

Clean It! Fix It! Eat It!

Joey Green's Magic Brands

The Mad Scientist Handbook 2

Senior Moments

Jesus and Moses: The Parallel Sayings

Joey Green's Amazing Kitchen Cures

Jesus and Muhammad: The Parallel Sayings

Joey Green's Gardening Magic

How They Met

Joey Green's Incredible Country Store

Potato Radio, Dizzy Dice

Contrary to Popular Belief

Weird Christmas

Marx & Lennon

THE PARALLEL SAYINGS

EDITED BY
Joey Green

FOREWORD BY
yoko ono

INTRODUCTION BY
Arthur Marx

NEW YORK

ISBN: 1-4013-0809-0

Hyperion books are available for special promotions and premiums. For details contact Michael Rentas, Assistant Director, Inventory Operations, Hyperion, 77 West 66th Street, 11th floor, New York, New York 10023-6298, or call 212-456-0133.

Book design by Richard Oriolo

FIRST EDITION

10 9 8 7 6 5 4 3 2 1

Contents

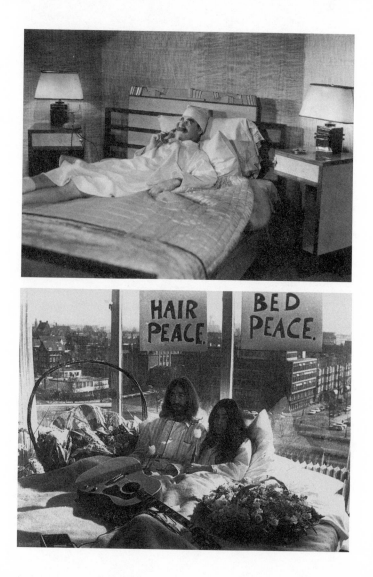

Foreword

by yoko ono

GROUCHO'S FAMOUS LINE, "I DON'T want to belong to any club that will accept me as a member," is so great that it makes me laugh each time I think about it. It's funny and deep: a statement of independence and rebellion against the bourgeois idea of "the privileged class."

Equally, John's statement, "There is a great woman behind every idiot," is something women of all walks of life will never forget. Like Groucho's remark, it's hilarious and at the same time casts a new light on the old concept of women in the male society.

Through humor, Groucho Marx turned people's heads around. John Lenin, excuse me, Lennon, shook the old system through his witticisms, and brought in the New Age.

I love the Parallel Sayings idea, which does not end with just proving how similar they were, but how wise each one was in his own right. John would get a laugh out of the fact that there is now a book comparing him to Groucho, whom he loved very much.

In this day and age when political correctness is in vogue, when nobody dares to say anything that is truly meaningful, the daring and wise remarks these two gutsy and reckless geniuses made are important to listen to again. As you turn the pages, this book will make you laugh and have fun. At the same time, it will plant a seed of revolution in your mind.

Introduction

by Arthur Marx

WHEN I WAS GROWING UP in the Twenties and thinking of a career for myself, my father, Groucho, used to lecture me, "Don't become an actor just because I am. It's a lousy life."

What he was referring to, of course, was his life as a struggling vaudevillian before he and his brothers made it big on Broadway in their first hit show, *I'll Say She Is,* which wowed the folks in Manhattan in 1924. His life after that was anything but lousy.

By 1929 Groucho was starring with his brothers Harpo, Chico, and Zeppo in his third hit Broadway show, *Animal Crackers,* and making about two grand a week. He was married to a beautiful woman, my mother, Ruth Johnson. He was living in a luxurious house in Great Neck, Long Island. He had two expensive cars in his garage. He had his suits made to order by Earl Bennam, one of the finest tailors on the island of Manhattan. He smoked the best Cuban cigars money could buy. And he worked nights, leaving the daylight hours free to entertain me, take me to Yankee baseball games, teach me how to play tennis, and get his own exercise trying to break ninety at Lakeville Country Club. He never did break ninety, but he did succeed in killing a swan or two on one of its water holes with his errant golf shots.

His friends were some of the most important figures in the world of sports, show business, literature, and politics— Eddie Cantor, Jack Dempsey, Ring Lardner, George Kaufman, Somerset Maugham, the Prince of Wales, F. Scott Fitzgerald, Babe Ruth, Charlie Chaplin, Alexander Woollcott, Al Smith (Governor of New York), Bobby Jones, Doug Fairbanks, Al Capone, and William Randolph Hearst.

I'm sure that John Lennon and the other Beatles would have been included in that mix if the Marx Brothers hadn't preceded the Beatles on the world stage by so many years. Groucho enjoyed hobnobbing with music geniuses— Andrés Segovia, George Gershwin, José Iturbi, and Oscar Levant, to name a few.

Groucho was crazy about music, whether it be classical or popular, and one of his biggest regrets in life was that when he was a kid his parents could only afford to give piano lessons to his brother Chico. Nevertheless he taught himself to play the piano and guitar by ear, and he had a good voice. Some of his most shining moments on stage and screen were his vocal renditions of "Hurray for Captain Spaulding," "Lydia the Tattooed Lady," and (with his brothers) "We're Four of the Three Musketeers" in *Animal Crackers*.

It's no coincidence that the Beatles have been likened by critics to the Marx Brothers in the way they electrified audiences with their fresh approach to comedy and song. And it's precisely for that reason that Groucho enjoyed them as entertainers as much as he did. "Because they're different and audacious," he told me. "There's nobody like them. Just like the Marx Brothers when we were in our prime. That's what makes the 'greats' great. My hat's off to them—even though I stopped wearing hats some time ago."

And, finally, Groucho would be flattered to know that so many years after the Marx Brothers first became legends the Beatles were being compared to them, and that he and Lennon would be doing a book together.

Parallel Sayings,
Parallel Lives

IN 1969, THE COMEDY GROUP Firesign Theatre—comprised of Phil Austin, Philip Proctor, Peter Bergman, and David Ossman—released their second record album, entitled *How Can You Be in Two Places at Once When You're Not Anywhere at All?* The cover of that album features side-by-side photos of Groucho Marx and John Lennon, over the headline (in mock Russian letters): All Hail Marx and Lennon.

While replacing the Soviet Union's founding fathers, Karl Marx and Vladimir Lenin, with Groucho Marx and John Lennon was a unique (and promising) idea, songwriter Irving Berlin had made a similar observation three years earlier. In a poem to Groucho for his birthday in 1966, Berlin wrote:

"The world would not be in such a snarl
If Marx had been Groucho instead of Karl."

Two years later, student protests at Nanterre in Paris in 1968 gave birth to the slogan *"Je suis Marxiste—tendance Groucho"* (I am a Marxist of the Groucho tendency).

Other people had also noticed the parallels between Groucho Marx and John Lennon.

In the *New York Times* of August 12, 1964, critic Bosley Crowther called the Beatles' first movie, *A Hard Day's Night,* a "fine conglomeration of madcap clowning in the old Marx Brothers' style." Movie critics hailed the Beatles in their second movie, *Help!,* as "modern Marx Brothers," and the Beatles themselves had prepared for their roles by studying the Marx Brothers movie *Duck Soup.*

For the cover of their landmark 1967 album, *Sgt. Pepper's Lonely Hearts Club Band,* the Beatles compiled a list of people they admired whose photographs would appear posed behind them. While comedians W. C. Fields, Stan Laurel, and Oliver Hardy appear on the album cover, Groucho Marx does not. Karl Marx, however, does.

In 1969, the same year that Firesign Theatre released their album featuring photographs of Marx and Lennon on the cover, British-based MacDonald Publishers issued *The Beatles Illustrated Lyrics,* a book edited by Alan Aldridge and featuring the lyrics to Beatles songs accompanied by striking illustrations by a wide range of contemporary artists. In that book, artist David King illustrated the lyrics to the Beatles' song "Revolution" with a photo collage of Karl Marx and John Lennon.

The lyrics to Don McLean's 1971 hit song "American Pie" whimsically describe Lennon reading a book on Marx, referring to either Groucho Marx (and John Lennon's propensity for creating similar wordplay in his lyrics and writings) or Karl Marx (and John Lennon's radical political activism).

In 1996, the International Collectors Society of Owings Mills, Maryland, ran advertisements in the United States offering a limited edition of two commemorative postage stamps featuring Groucho Marx and John Lennon, allegedly issued by the Republic of Abkhazia—a former "autonomous region" within the Soviet Union. Most philatelic experts regard the stamps, unusable in Abkhazia, as a hoax perpetrated by the company to create bootleg merchandise under the auspices of a small third world country.

All of this raises an interesting question: Is there a deeper correlation between Groucho Marx and John Lennon?

Consider these startling coincidences:

- Both men were born in October—exactly fifty years apart.

- Groucho founded the Marx Brothers act; John Lennon founded the Beatles.

- There were originally five Marx Brothers (Groucho, Chico, Harpo, Zeppo, and Gummo); there were originally five Beatles (John Lennon, Paul McCartney, George Harrison, Stuart Sutcliffe, and Pete Best).

- Groucho was known as the witty Marx Brother; John Lennon was known as the witty Beatle.

- Groucho Marx was born in New York City; John Lennon died in New York City.

- Both the Marx Brothers and the Beatles originally billed themselves as singing groups.

- Groucho Marx starred with his brothers in *A Night at the Opera*; John Lennon starred with the Beatles in *A Hard Day's Night*.

- Groucho Marx wrote the book *Beds*, featuring pictures of himself in bed; for their honeymoon in 1969, John Lennon and Yoko Ono staged a weeklong "Bed-In" for peace at the Amsterdam Hilton, allowing the press to take pictures of them in bed.

- Both men wore Windsor eyeglasses, grew a moustache, smoked, played guitar, and sang.

- Groucho played the leader of the country Freedonia; John declared himself a citizen of the country Nutopia.

- Groucho frequently referred to himself as Dr. Hugo Hackenbush; John Lennon frequently referred to himself as Dr. Winston O'Boogie.

- Groucho appeared as an animated character in Warner Brothers cartoons; John Lennon appeared as an animated character in Saturday morning cartoons.

- Groucho played Carnegie Hall for one night to a sold-out audience; John Lennon played Carnegie Hall with the Beatles for one night to a sold-out audience.

- The French government bestowed upon Groucho the French Legion of Honor *Commandeur dans l'Ordre des Arts et des Lettres*; Queen Elizabeth bestowed upon John Lennon an MBE— "Membership of the Most Excellent Order of the British Empire."

- Groucho guest-hosted *The Tonight Show* for a week; John and Yoko guest-hosted *The Mike Douglas Show* for a week.

- Both men appeared twice on the cover of *Time* magazine, once with their group and later alone.

- Both men guest-starred on *The Dick Cavett Show,* were interviewed by *Playboy,* won Academy Awards, and have stars on the Hollywood Walk of Fame.

- Groucho had three children (Arthur, Miriam, and Melinda); John Lennon had three children (Julian, step-daughter Kyoko, and Sean).

- Both men broke up the acts that made them famous.

The similarities don't stop there.

Outsiders gave both Groucho and John a key element of their show business persona. Stand-up comedian Art Fisher nicknamed the Marx Brothers, giving them all stage names with the suffix –o; German photographer Astrid Kirchherr gave the Beatles their signature mop-top haircuts.

Both Groucho and John stirred controversy. In an interview with Maureen Cleave in 1966, John Lennon said the Beatles were more popular than Jesus, prompting radio stations across the Bible Belt to urge listeners to burn the Beatles' albums; during a taping of his radio show, *You Bet Your Life,* Groucho told a woman contestant with twenty-two children, "I love my cigar too, but I take it out of my mouth once in a while," prompting director Robert Dwan to censor the racy quip from the tape.

Both Groucho Marx and John Lennon appeared naked in public.

In 1935, MGM studio chief Irving Thalberg ushered the Marx Brothers into his office for a meeting at the appointed time but was soon called away on urgent business. He returned to discover the Marx Brothers in his office, naked, roasting potatoes in his office fireplace.

In 1968, John Lennon and Yoko Ono released a record album entitled *Two Virgins*, featuring a cover photograph of the two of them standing naked, facing the camera.

Both John Lennon and Groucho Marx dropped acid.

In 1967, shortly after the release of their psychedelic album *Sgt. Pepper's Lonely Hearts Club Band*, John admitted that he had used LSD and later claimed that he had dropped acid thousands of times.

Paul Krassner, founder and publisher of *The Realist*, swears that he took LSD as a guide with Groucho Marx. In "My Acid Trip with Groucho," published in the February 1981 issue of *High Times*, Krassner claimed that Groucho, preparing for a role in the psychedelic 1968 Otto Preminger film *Skidoo*, asked him to get some LSD and accompany him on the trip. Krassner told me, "As far as I know, that was the only time he took acid, and I suspect Lennon was exaggerating when he said thousands of times, but ya never know."

The FBI considered both Groucho Marx and John Lennon

as potential threats to the United States government and kept extensive files on both men.

In 1953, prompted by an informant who accused Groucho of being a member of the Communist Party, the FBI began monitoring the comedian's television and radio broadcasts. The 243-page file, declassified by the FBI in 1998, contains letters from upset viewers of Groucho's television game show *You Bet Your Life*. One letter complained that Groucho had referred to the United States as "the United Snakes." Agents wrote internal memorandums analyzing the subversive content of Groucho's jokes, ultimately dismissing the sarcastic comments as harmless to national security. By the early 1960s, the FBI concluded that Groucho was not a member of the Communist Party and closed the file.

The FBI also monitored John Lennon. According to a secret memo declassified in 2000, a "confidential source" warned the FBI that the former Beatle planned to organize political rallies against President Richard Nixon's 1972 reelection campaign, culminating in a massive peace demonstration at the Republican National Convention. The memo urged the Nixon administration to deport Lennon as "a strategy counter-measure." South Carolina Republican Senator Strom Thurmond sent a copy of that secret memo to United States Attorney General John Mitchell, and the following month, the Immigration and Naturalization Service began deportation proceedings against Lennon based on his 1968 marijuana possession conviction in London and ordered him to leave the United States within two months. At the instruction of FBI director J. Edgar Hoover, FBI agents attended Lennon's concerts, scrutinized his song lyrics, tapped his telephone, and tailed him. Unable to find any evidence of criminal wrongdoing, the FBI suggested setting up Lennon for another drug bust so he could be deported immediately. In 1975, the U.S. Court of Appeals barred the deportation order, voided Lennon's drug conviction, reprimanded the Nixon administration, and praised Lennon's efforts to remain in the country as "testimony to his faith in the American dream." A year later, Lennon received his green card.

All these astounding similarities between Groucho Marx and John Lennon beg the question: Did Groucho and John ever meet? Were they familiar with each other's work? Did they recognize each other as kindred spirits?

At a Beatles press conference in Sydney, Australia, on June 11, 1964, a reporter asked, "You've been likened with the likes of the Marx Brothers. Do you find this a compliment?" John Lennon replied, "Yeah, it's a compliment. They're funny, aren't they?"

Groucho Marx did attend the Beatles concert at the Hollywood Bowl on August 23, 1964. The next day, the Beatles helped raise $10,000 for the Hemophilia Foundation of Southern California by appearing (not performing) at a Brentwood garden soiree hosted by Capitol Records. The Fab Four sat on stools and greeted guests, including five hundred celebrities and their relatives: Edward G. Robinson, Lloyd Bridges, Rita Hayworth, Eva Marie Saint, and Groucho Marx. In his autobiography, Bob Eubanks, who promoted the Beatles' Hollywood Bowl concert, recalls that Groucho quipped to reporters that he was only at the garden soiree to "get drunk."

While in London that same year, Groucho took his third wife, Eden Hartford, and their daughter Melinda to see *A Hard Day's Night.* "Halfway through, I wandered to the men's room and suddenly found myself in a pub across the street, drinking nut brown ale and singing 'The Whiffenpoof Song' to a stunned and incredulous crowd," wrote Groucho in a letter dated September 16, 1964. "My criticism of the Beatles picture is that it is sans jokes. Lunacy is not necessarily comedy."

In October 1973, John separated from Yoko and moved to Los Angeles with his personal assistant and companion May Pang to embark on what he later called his "Lost Weekend"—eighteen months of wild partying in the company of Keith Moon, Ringo Starr, Klaus Voormann, and Harry Nilsson. During this time, Groucho also lived in Los Angeles. "While John and I were in Los Angeles," May Pang told me, "we never got together with Groucho Marx."

Just as the lives of Groucho Marx and John Lennon teem with distinct parallels, the similarities between their witticisms are equally intriguing. At their core, Groucho and John were highly imaginative individuals who shared an acerbic, anarchic wit and a quirky comic sensibility. Both men innately expressed a healthy disdain for haughty pretense, cheeky defiance in the face of misplaced piety, and a keen skepticism—peppered with clever non sequiturs and ingenious wordplay.

The quotes in this book attributed to Groucho Marx are culled from Marx Brothers movie dialogue, books and articles written by Groucho, songs sung by Groucho, television appearances, radio shows, and interviews. I have also included several quotes widely attributed to Groucho. Although I could not locate sources for these attributed sayings, Groucho's son Arthur has identified them as authentic.

The quotes in the book attributed to John Lennon are taken from song lyrics (both collaborative and solo work), dialogue from Beatles movies, books and writings by John Lennon, interviews, and press conferences. I limited the lyrics from Beatles songs written by John Lennon and Paul McCartney solely to those where John Lennon claimed sole authorship or significant involvement.

Here then for the first time—placed on the same page for easy comparison—are the sayings and writings of Groucho

Marx and the parallel sayings, lyrics, and writings of John Lennon. Fans of Groucho Marx and the Marx Brothers will be amazed to discover how deftly John Lennon's lyrics and writings echo the witticisms of Groucho Marx. Fans of John Lennon and the Beatles will be awed to discover how remarkably John Lennon's lyrics, writings, and quips match the wit and irreverence expressed by Groucho Marx in his writings and in Marx Brothers movies. These quotes clearly show that Groucho Marx and John Lennon were highly gifted individuals who shared an unusual and delightful perspective on life, spreading laughter and joy throughout the world. Through humor and song, Groucho and John made a greater and more enduring impact on civilization than the Soviet Union's founding fathers could have ever dreamed possible. When it comes to influencing generations, Karl Marx and Vladimir Lenin don't hold a candle to Groucho Marx and John Lennon.

All Hail Marx and Lennon!

—JOEY GREEN

The Parallel Sayings

Marx

Since I plan on seeing you in the not too distant future,
I'll knock this off with a hey nonny nonny and a hotcha-
cha. That's what people were saying around Paramount
in 1930—and we sneer at the Beatles!

—*THE GROUCHO LETTERS*

★

Lennon

If only everything were as simple and unaffected
as McCartney's new single "My Love," then
maybe Dean Martin and Jerry Lewis would be
reunited with the Marx Brothers. . . .

—STATEMENT FROM JOHN AND YOKO
1973

Marx

I sent the club a wire stating, PLEASE ACCEPT MY RESIGNA-
TION. I DON'T WANT TO BELONG TO ANY CLUB THAT WILL ACCEPT
ME AS A MEMBER.

—*GROUCHO AND ME*

★

Lennon

I am returning my MBE in protest against
Britain's involvement in the Nigeria-Biafra thing,
against our support of America in Vietnam, and
against "Cold Turkey" slipping down in the
charts.

—LETTER TO THE QUEEN
NOVEMBER 25, 1969

Marx

We've come a long way to entertain you. The least you
could do is throw silver.

—During a 1922 performance of *On the Balcony* at the Coliseum Theatre in London when the English Audience Started Throwing Pennies on the Stage, according to *The Groucho Phile*

Lennon

Those in the cheaper seats clap. The rest of you
rattle your jewelry.

—Royal Variety Performance
November 15, 1963

Marx

I never forget a face, but in your case I'll be glad to make
an exception.

—ATTRIBUTED

★

Lennon

Instant Karma's gonna get you,
Gonna look you right in the face.
You better get yourself together darlin',
Join the human race.

—"INSTANT KARMA!"

Marx

[He] may look like an idiot and talk like an idiot but don't let that fool you. He really is an idiot.

—*DUCK SOUP*

★

Lennon

He who laughs last is usually the dumbest kid on the block.

—*SKYWRITING BY WORD OF MOUTH*

Marx

Believe me, you've got to get up early if you want to get out of bed.

—*THE COCOANUTS*

★

Lennon

She told me she worked in the morning and
    started to laugh.
I told her I didn't and crawled up to sleep in
    the bath.

—"NORWEGIAN WOOD"
BY JOHN LENNON AND PAUL MCCARTNEY

Marx

I made a killing on Wall Street a few years ago . . . I shot my broker.

—To an Economist
on *You Bet Your Life*

★

Lennon

Hey Bungalow Bill,
What did you kill,
Bungalow Bill?

—"The Continuing Story of Bungalow Bill"
by John Lennon and Paul McCartney

Marx

Why, you're one of the most beautiful women I've ever seen, and that's not saying much for you.

—Animal Crackers

★

Lennon

For what she lacked in passion, she made up for in gardening.

—Skywriting by Word of Mouth

Marx

Wives are people who feel they don't dance enough.

—Memoirs of a Mangy Lover

★

Lennon

I don't need to hug or hold you tight,
I just want to dance with you all night;
In this world there's nothing I would rather do,
'Cause I'm happy just to dance with you.

—"I'm Happy Just to Dance with You"
BY John Lennon and Paul McCartney

Marx

I haven't eaten in three days. I didn't eat yesterday,
I didn't eat today, and I'm not going to eat tomorrow.
That makes it three days.

—*MONKEY BUSINESS*

★

Lennon

One and one and one is three.
Got to be good looking cause he's so hard to see.

—"COME TOGETHER"
BY JOHN LENNON AND PAUL MCCARTNEY

Marx

Military intelligence is a contradiction in terms.

—ATTRIBUTED

Lennon

We're playing those mind games together
Pushing the barriers, planting seeds
Playing the mind guerrilla
Chanting the mantra peace on earth.

—"MIND GAMES"

Marx

I'm not feeling very well, I need a doctor immediately.
Ring the nearest golf course.

—*I'll Say She Is!*

★

Lennon

When you're drowning, you don't say, "I would
be incredibly pleased if someone would have the
foresight to notice me drowning and come and
help me." You just *scream*.

—*Lennon Remembers*

Marx

Well, we've got to speed things up. Chef, if a guest orders a three-minute egg, give it to him in two minutes. If he orders a two-minute egg, give it to him in one minute. And if he orders a one-minute egg, give him a chicken and let him work it out for himself.

—*A Night in Casablanca*

Lennon

I am the eggman, they are the eggmen, I am the walrus.

—"I Am the Walrus"
 by John Lennon and Paul McCartney

Marx

From the moment I picked your book up until I laid it down, I was convulsed with laughter. Someday I intend reading it.

—BACK COVER BLURB FOR THE 1928 BOOK
DAWN GINSBERG'S REVENGE
BY S. J. PERELMAN

★

Lennon

[He] should stick to dancing, which he's also not good at.

—*SKYWRITING BY WORD OF MOUTH*

Marx

I love my cigar too, but I take it out of my mouth once in a while.

—To a woman contestant with twenty-two children
during the taping of *You Bet Your Life*

★

Lennon

Don't play the Virgin Mary
We all know you've been screwed.

—"Rock 'n' Roll People"

Marx

We took pictures of the native girls, but they weren't
developed. But we're going back again in a couple of
weeks.

—*ANIMAL CRACKERS*

★

Lennon

REPORTER: You've been getting more
   and more gifts from fans. What was
   the most unusual gift you've ever
   received? . . .

JOHN: I once received a bra . . . with "I Love John"
   embroidered on it. I thought it was pretty original. I didn't keep it, mind you. It didn't fit.

—INTERVIEW BY LARRY KANE
   SEPTEMBER 13, 1964

Marx

One false move and I'm yours.

—*THE COCOANUTS*

Lennon

It won't be long—yeah, yeah.
It won't be long—yeah, yeah.
It won't be long—yeah, yeah.
Till I belong to you.

—"IT WON'T BE LONG"
BY JOHN LENNON AND PAUL MCCARTNEY

Marx

I must say I find television very educational. The minute somebody turns it on, I go into the library and read a good book.

—"KING LEER"

★

Lennon

If everyone demanded peace instead of another TV set, we'd have peace.

—PRESS CONFERENCE
ONTARIO SCIENCE CENTRE
TORONTO, CANADA
DECEMBER 17, 1969

Marx

ZEPPO: Anything further, father?

GROUCHO: "Anything further, father?" That can't be right. Isn't it "anything farther, further?"

—HORSE FEATHERS

★

Lennon

It wasn't long before old dad
Was cumbersome—a drag.
He seemed to get the message and
Began to pack his bag.
"You don't want me around," he said,
"I'm old and crippled too."
We didn't have the heart to say
"You're bloody right it's true."

—A SPANIARD IN THE WORKS

Marx

Time flies like an arrow. Fruit flies like a banana.

—ATTRIBUTED

★

Lennon

He was fond of fruitlessness. This he would eat
every morning unusually mixed with a yogurt.

—*SKYWRITING BY WORD OF MOUTH*

Marx

I danced before Napoleon. No, Napoleon danced before me. In fact, he danced two hundred years before me.

—*Duck Soup*

Lennon

And of course,
Henry the Horse
Dances the waltz.

—"Being for the Benefit of Mr. Kite"
by John Lennon and Paul McCartney

Marx

Although it is generally known, I think it's about time to announce that I was born at a very early age.

—*GROUCHO AND ME*

★

Lennon

I kept pretty much to myself most of my life—
I never knew when I might need me.

—*SKYWRITING BY WORD OF MOUTH*

Marx

Imagine if horse racing had no horses—thousands of people could go to the track each day and save millions of dollars.

—Untitled column for *Variety*

★

Lennon

Imagine there's no heaven,
It's easy if you try,
No hell below us,
Above us only sky.

—"Imagine"

Marx

If I hold you any closer, I'll be in back of you.

—*A Day at the Races*

★

Lennon

Hold me tight,
Tell me I'm the only one,
And then I might
Never be the lonely one.

—"Hold Me Tight"
by John Lennon and Paul McCartney

Marx

One morning I shot an elephant in my pajamas. How he got in my pajamas I don't know.

—*ANIMAL CRACKERS*

★

Lennon

"You're just in time," the cow said,
Its eyes were all aglaze,
"I'm feeling like an elephant,
I aren't been milked for days."
"Why is this," I asked it,
Tugging at its throttles.
"I don't know why, perhaps it's 'cause
MY milk comes out in bottles."

—*A SPANIARD IN THE WORKS*

Marx

Is it true you're getting a divorce as soon as your husband recovers his eyesight?

—*MONKEY BUSINESS*

★

Lennon

Living is easy with eyes closed,
Misunderstanding all you see.
It's getting hard to be someone
But it all works out,
It doesn't matter much to me.

—"STRAWBERRY FIELDS FOREVER"
BY JOHN LENNON AND PAUL MCCARTNEY

Marx

The truth is, if a young man doesn't like girls it is more
than likely that eventually an analyst will tell him
(I mean after four years at thirty-five dollars a throw)
that he is either in love with his mother, his father, or the
boy next door.

—*MEMOIRS OF A MANGY LOVER*

★

Lennon

Why make it sad to be gay?
Doing your thing is okay.
Our body's our own, so leave us alone
And play with yourself today.

—*THE GAY LIBERATION BOOK*

Marx

So, don't be too envious of the rich man, sitting in the back of his Rolls Royce, swathed in a raccoon coat, with a beautiful blonde on his arm. How does he know that she loves him for himself alone, and is not just after his fur coat?

—*Many Happy Returns*

Lennon

Say you don't need no diamond ring and I'll be
    satisfied,
Tell me that you want the kind of things that
    money just can't buy.

—"Can't Buy Me Love"
by John Lennon and Paul McCartney

Marx

Well, we've gone this far. We might as well go through with it.

—WHEN ASKED BY THE MINISTER IF HE WOULD TAKE
RUTH JOHNSON TO BE HIS LAWFUL WEDDED WIFE
AT THEIR WEDDING ON FEBRUARY 4, 1920,
ACCORDING TO *MY LIFE WITH GROUCHO*
BY ARTHUR MARX

★

Lennon

How can we go forward when we don't know which way we're facing?

—"HOW?"

Marx

The next time I see you, remind me not to talk to you.

—*The Cocoanuts*

★

Lennon

A conspiracy of silence speaks louder than words.

—*Skywriting by Word of Mouth*

Marx

You're quite a dish, Marie, and since I'm the head dish around here, let's start cooking.

—You Bet Your Life

★

Lennon

Well I'm cookin'
Just a cookin'
Cookin' in the kitchen of love
Cookin' in the kitchen of life
Lord, Lord, ain't nothin' to it
Come on and do it—cookin'.

—"Cookin' (in the Kitchen of Love)"

Marx

Don't look now, but there's one man too many in this room, and I think it's you.

—*Duck Soup*

★

Lennon

He's a real Nowhere Man,
Living in his Nowhere Land,
Making all his Nowhere plans for nobody.

—"Nowhere Man"
by John Lennon and Paul McCartney

Marx

You've got the brain of a four-year-old boy, and I'll bet he was glad to get rid of it.

—*Horse Feathers*

Lennon

I call my budgie Jeffrey
My grandads name's the same
I call him after grandad
Who had a feathered brain.

—*A Spaniard in the Works*

Marx

Goodbye for now and all my love and kisses to you—
well, most of them, anyhow.

—*Love, Groucho*

★

Lennon

I'll pretend I am kissing,
The lips I am missing,
And hope that my dreams will come true.
And then while I'm away,
I'll write home every day,
And I'll send all my loving to you.

—"All My Loving"
by John Lennon and Paul McCartney

Marx

I'm a different man behind a desk, as any stenographer can tell you.

—*A Night in Casablanca*

★

Lennon

"A man in my position," he whispered from between her legs, "can't afford the publicity."

—*Skywriting by Word of Mouth*

Marx

Well, I could go on like this for days but I know you're a busy man, playing with that toilet plunger, and I don't want to keep you from your work.

—*THE GROUCHO LETTERS*

★

Lennon

I don't expect you to understand,
After you caused so much pain,
But then again you're not to blame,
You're just a human, a victim of the insane.

—"ISOLATION"

Marx

CHICO: I've seen you someplace before.

GROUCHO: Well, I don't know where I was, but I'll stay out of there in the future.

—*ANIMAL CRACKERS*

★

Lennon

I won't want to stay,
I don't have much to say,
But I can turn away,
And you won't see me.

—"YOU WON'T SEE ME"
BY JOHN LENNON AND PAUL MCCARTNEY

Marx

If he doesn't behave himself, I'll buy this hotel and make him a bellhop. No, that's too good for him. I'll make him a guest.

—*ROOM SERVICE*

★

Lennon

You've got to live
You've got to love
You've got to be somebody
You've got to shove
But it's so hard, it's really hard
Sometimes I feel like going down.

—"IT'S SO HARD"

Marx

I never realized what dull company I was until I sat there alone. I had heard everything I had to say time and time again, and I was in no mood to listen to me again.

—*Memoirs of a Mangy Lover*

★

Lennon

What have I done to deserve myself?

—*Skywriting by Word of Mouth*

Marx

Age is not a particularly interesting subject. Anyone can get old. All you have to do is live long enough.

—*Groucho and Me*

★

Lennon

They say life begins at forty;
Age is just a state of mind.
If all that's true, you know
That I've been dead for thirty-nine.

—"Life Begins at 40"

Marx

It's women like you that make men like me like women like you.

—I'll Say She Is!

★

Lennon

I get high when I see you go by—my oh my.

—"It's Only Love"
by John Lennon and Paul McCartney

Marx

I'll bet your father spent the first year of your life
throwing rocks at the stork.

—*At the Circus*

★

Lennon

As soon as you're born they make you feel small,
By giving you no time instead of it all,
Till the pain is so big you feel nothing at all.

—"Working Class Hero"

Marx

My favorite poem is the one that starts "Thirty days hath
September" because it actually tells you something.

—ATTRIBUTED

Lennon

Amonk amink a minibus,
Amarmylaidie Moon,
Amikky mendip multiplus
Amighty midgey spoon.

—*IN HIS OWN WRITE*

Marx

I haven't room enough in here to swing a cat. In fact, I haven't even got a cat.

—*MONKEY BUSINESS*

★

Lennon

If you can manicure a cat, can you caticure a man?

—*SKYWRITING BY WORD OF MOUTH*

Marx

So, if all you men will leave the room, I'll tell this lovely young thing sitting next to me, this wanton waif, all about Poughkeepsie.

—BEDS

★

Lennon

While the swine's away the piglets can play.

—A HARD DAY'S NIGHT

Marx

You can leave in a taxi. If you can't get a taxi, you can leave in a huff. If that's too soon, you can leave in a minute and a huff.

—*Duck Soup*

★

Lennon

Newspaper taxis appear by the shore
Waiting to take you away
Climb in the back with your head in the clouds
And you're gone.

—"Lucy in the Sky with Diamonds"
by John Lennon and Paul McCartney

Marx

Well, Art is Art, isn't it? Still, on the other hand, water is water! And East is East and West is West and if you take cranberries and stew them like applesauce they taste much more like prunes than rhubarb does.

—*ANIMAL CRACKERS*

★

Lennon

East is east and west is west,
The twain shall meet.
East is west and west is east,
Let it be complete.

—"YOU ARE HERE"

Marx

A man in my position (horizontal at the moment) is likely to hear strange stories about himself. A few years ago they were saying that I made a pig out of myself drinking champagne out of Miss Garbo's slipper. Actually it was nothing but very weak punch.

—"My Best Friend Is a Dog . . ."

★

Lennon

Christ! You know it ain't easy.
You know how hard it can be.
The way things are going,
They're going to crucify me.

—"The Ballad of John and Yoko"
by John Lennon and Paul McCartney

Marx

I had no idea that this war would disturb my private life
and I may have to write a letter to the *London Times*.

—*THE GROUCHO LETTERS*

★

Lennon

The world stage was soon to reopen with a
revival of World War One. It was to be known as
World War Two.

—*SKYWRITING BY WORD OF MOUTH*

Marx

Three years ago I came to Florida without a nickel in my
pocket. Now I have a nickel in my pocket.

—*The Cocoanuts*

★

Lennon

REPORTER: What will you do when Beatlemania
  subsides?
JOHN: Count the money.

—Press conference
  North America
  1965

Marx

I intend to live forever, or die trying.

—ATTRIBUTED

★

Lennon

They lived hopefully ever after, and who could
blame them?

—"JOCK AND YONO"

Marx

What other hobbies you got?

—To a man with twelve children
in *The Big Store*

★

Lennon

"Love is never having to pull yourself together,"
she said quite suddenly. "Love is never having to
pull yourself off," he replied in a lighter vein.

—*Skywriting by Word of Mouth*

Marx

You have a very good head on your shoulders, and I wish it were on mine.

—To a pretty girl
on *You Bet Your Life*

★

Lennon

If the sun has faded away,

I'll try to make it shine,

There is nothing I won't do.

If you need a shoulder to cry on,

I hope it will be mine,

Call me tonight and I'll come to you.

—"Any Time at All"
by John Lennon and Paul McCartney

Marx

Sir, are you trying to offer me a bribe? How much?

—*MONKEY BUSINESS*

★

Lennon

REPORTER: Will you please sing something?
JOHN: No, we need money first.

—PRESS CONFERENCE
NEW YORK'S KENNEDY AIRPORT
FEBRUARY 7, 1964

Marx

SECRETARY: Sir, you try my patience.

GROUCHO: I don't mind if I do. You must come over and
try mine sometime.

—*DUCK SOUP*

★

Lennon

Would you believe in a love at first sight?
Yes, I'm certain that it happens all the time.
What do you see when you turn out the light?
I can't tell you but I know it's mine.

—"WITH A LITTLE HELP FROM MY FRIENDS"
BY JOHN LENNON AND PAUL McCARTNEY

Marx

Where are we going to get two thousand dollars? I'll tell
you what. If you two will each put up a thousand dollars,
I'll put up the balance.

—*Flywheel, Shyster, and Flywheel*

★

Lennon

If you want money for people with minds that hate,
All I can tell you is brother you'll have to wait.

—"Revolution"
by John Lennon and Paul McCartney

Marx

ZEPPO: The garbage man is here.

GROUCHO: Tell him we don't want any.

—*HOME AGAIN*

★

Lennon

I have enough of my own garbage, never mind dealing with other people's.

—*SKYWRITING BY WORD OF MOUTH*

Marx

I'm sick of these conventional marriages. One woman
and one man was good enough for your grandmother,
but who wants to marry your grandmother? Nobody, not
even your grandfather.

—Animal Crackers

★

Lennon

From Liverpool to Tokyo,
What a way to go.
From distant lands,
One woman, one man.
Let the four winds blow.

—"You Are Here"

Marx

One day I looked myself in the eye—not an easy trick
with bifocals.

—"How to Build a Secret Weapon"

★

Lennon

One way of looking at it is simply not to look at it
at all.

—"The Great Wok"

Marx

Take, for example, "Early to bed, early to rise, makes
a man you-know-what." This is a lot of hoopla. Most
wealthy people I know like to sleep late, and will fire the
help if they are disturbed before three in the afternoon.
Pray tell (I cribbed that from *Little Women*), who are the
people who get up at the crack of dawn? Policemen, fire-
men, garbage collectors, bus drivers, department store
clerks and others in the lower income bracket. You don't
see Marilyn Monroe getting up at six in the morning.
The truth is, I don't see Marilyn getting up at any hour,
more's the pity.

—*Groucho and Me*

★

Lennon

When I wake up early in the morning,
Lift my head, I'm still yawning;
When I'm in the middle of a dream,
Stay in bed, float upstream.
Please don't wake me,
No, don't shake me;
Leave me where I am,
I'm only sleeping.

—"I'M ONLY SLEEPING"
BY JOHN LENNON AND PAUL MCCARTNEY

Marx

Paying alimony is like feeding hay to a dead horse.

—ATTRIBUTED

★

Lennon

You can't pull strings if your hands are tied.

—"STEEL AND GLASS"

Marx

I don't know why, but whenever I dream of a nurse she always has red hair. Red hair makes a man want to recover his health quickly, so that he can get on his feet and the nurse off hers.

—*THE GROUCHO LETTERS*

★

Lennon

Help me if you can, I'm feeling down
And I do appreciate you being round.
Help me get my feet back on the ground,
Won't you please, please help me.

—"HELP"
BY JOHN LENNON AND PAUL MCCARTNEY

Marx

Either he's dead or my watch has stopped.

—*A Day at the Races*

★

Lennon

Perhaps life's Karmic Wheel had bent his
spokes.

—*Skywriting by Word of Mouth*

Marx

People stopped inviting me to their homes—the same
people who hadn't been inviting me for years.

—Memoirs of a Mangy Lover

Lennon

REPORTER: The French have not made up their
    minds about the Beatles. What do you think of
    them?
JOHN: Oh, we like the Beatles.

    —Press conference
    Paris, France
    January 14, 1964

Marx

If you run out of gas, get ethyl. If Ethyl runs out, get
Mabel.

—*Duck Soup*

★

Lennon

I told that girl she could start right away,
And she said, listen, babe, I've got something to say,
I've got no car, and it's breaking my heart,
But I found a driver and that's a start.

—"Drive My Car"
by John Lennon and Paul McCartney

Marx

I know you work hard for your money—at least when the boss is looking.

—MANY HAPPY RETURNS

★

Lennon

Everybody's hustlin' for a buck and a dime
I'll scratch your back and you knife mine.

—"NOBODY LOVES YOU (WHEN YOU'RE DOWN AND OUT)"

Marx

This [bill] is an outrage. If I were you, I wouldn't pay it.

—*A Night at the Opera*

★

Lennon

It's a long way to tip a waiter.

—*Skywriting by Word of Mouth*

Marx

A man is as old as the woman he feels.

—*THE SECRET WORD IS GROUCHO*

Lennon

And when I touch you I feel happy inside,
It's such a feeling that my love I can't hide.

—"I WANT TO HOLD YOUR HAND"
BY JOHN LENNON AND PAUL MCCARTNEY

Marx

One for all and all for me and me for you and three for five and six for a quarter.

—*THE COCOANUTS*

★

Lennon

I am me as you are he as you are me and we are all together.

—"I AM THE WALRUS"
BY JOHN LENNON AND PAUL MCCARTNEY

Marx

This would be a better world for children if the parents
had to eat the spinach.

—*Animal Crackers*

★

Lennon

This would be a holiday if I wasn't working.

—*Skywriting by Word of Mouth*

Marx

Those are my principles. If you don't like them I have others.

—Attributed

★

Lennon

People asking questions, lost in confusion,
Well I tell them there's no problem, only
   solutions.

—"Watching the Wheels"

Marx

It's kind of nice to be married again, except that I can't stop making passes at strange girls. Of course this will eventually wear off, I imagine about the time I get divorced again.

—*THE GROUCHO LETTERS*

★

Lennon

Do you take this woman anywhere in particular?

—*SKYWRITING BY WORD OF MOUTH*

Marx

Lydia, oh Lydia,
Say, have you met Lydia?
Oh, Lydia, the tattooed lady.
She has eyes that folks adore so,
And a torso even more so.
Lydia, oh Lydia,
That "encyclopidia."
Oh, Lydia, the queen of tattoo.
On her back is the Battle of Waterloo.
Beside it the Wreck of the Hesperus too.
And proudly above waves the red, white, and blue.
You can learn a lot from Lydia.

—"LYDIA, THE TATTOOED LADY"
BY E. Y. HARBURG AND HAROLD ARLEN

★

Lennon

Well you should see Polythene Pam
She's so good-looking but she looks like a man
Well you should see her in drag dressed in her
    polythene bag
Yes you should see Polythene Pam
Yeah yeah yeah
Get a dose of her in jackboots and kilt
She's killer-diller when she's dressed to the hilt
She's the kind of a girl that makes the "News of
    the World"
Yes you could say she was attractively built
Yeah yeah yeah.

—"POLYTHENE PAM"
BY JOHN LENNON AND PAUL McCARTNEY

Marx

Your father is a meat distributor? Well, if you're any
indication, he certainly knows his business.

> —To a curvaceous woman
> on *You Bet Your Life*

★

Lennon

> Just a$ tight a$ you can make it,
> Hard and slow ain't hard enough,
> Just a$ tight a$ you can shake it girl,
> Git it on and do your stuff.

> —"Tight A$"

Marx

You know you haven't stopped talking since I came here? You must have been vaccinated with a phonograph needle.

—*Duck Soup*

★

Lennon

Words are flying out like endless rain into a
  paper cup,
They slither while, they pass, they slip away
  across the universe.

—"Across the Universe"
  by John Lennon and Paul McCartney

Marx

I knew one boy who had fallen arches. His mother took him to the doctor. That eminent physician, having no cure for fallen arches but desperately in need of some extra money for another year at medical school, removed his tonsils. The mother was so grateful for the removal of her son's tonsils that, as an added attraction, she allowed him to take out her appendix. Some months later, he took her out. She even paid for that, but that's another story.

—*MEMOIRS OF A MANGY LOVER*

Lennon

She said she loved me but I knew she was lying,
Felt like an Arab who was dancing through Zion,
Don't call no doctor when you just feel like crying,
It's all down to Goodnight Vienna.

—"GOODNIGHT VIENNA"

Marx

You know what a chaperone is—That's a French word meaning, "Brother, are you in for a dull evening!"

—*THE GROUCHO PHILE*

★

Lennon

I'm stuck inside of a lexicon with the Roget's Thesaurus Blues again.

—"SATIRE 2"

Marx

Madam, before I get through with you, you'll have a clear
case for divorce, and so will my wife.

—*MONKEY BUSINESS*

★

Lennon

I once had a girl or should I say she once had me.

—"NORWEGIAN WOOD"
BY JOHN LENNON AND PAUL MCCARTNEY

Marx

When I was your age, I went to bed right after supper. Sometimes I went to bed before supper. Sometimes I went without my supper and didn't go to bed at all.

—*HORSE FEATHERS*

★

Lennon

Well I can dish it out,
But I just can't take it . . .
Well I can sing for my supper,
But I just can't make it.

—"I DON'T WANNA FACE IT"

Marx

Love is a many-splendored thing. I don't quite know what this means, but songwriters have to make a living, too.

—Groucho and Me

★

Lennon

There's nothing you can know that isn't known,
Nothing you can see that isn't shown,
Nowhere you can be that isn't where you're
    meant to be—it's easy.
All you need is love.
All you need is love.
All you need is love.
Love is all you need.

—"All You Need Is Love"
by John Lennon and Paul McCartney

Marx

GROUCHO: How long have you been married?

WOMAN: Three wonderful years.

GROUCHO: Never mind the wonderful years. How many miserable years have you had?

—*YOU BET YOUR LIFE*

★

Lennon

I'm in love for the first time,
Don't you know it's going to last,
It's a love that lasts forever,
It's a love that has no past.

—"DON'T LET ME DOWN"
BY JOHN LENNON AND PAUL MCCARTNEY

Marx

The temptation of a beautiful woman can be your downfall—if you're lucky.

—"How to Be a Spy"

★

Lennon

And woman I will try to express
My inner feelings and thankfulness
For showing me the meaning of success.

—"Woman"

Marx

Now I want you to make two carbon copies of that letter
and throw the original away. And when you get through
with that, throw the carbon copies away. Just send the
stamp, airmail.

—Animal Crackers

★

Lennon

Dear World,

I think we should have peace. Why don't we
have it? I would like it today—so would my wife.

—"Dear World Letter"
1970

Marx

Behind every successful man stands a woman. Behind her stands his wife.

—ATTRIBUTED

★

Lennon

As usual, there is a great woman behind every idiot.

—AFTER RECEIVING HIS GREEN CARD FROM THE
UNITED STATES IMMIGRATION AND NATURALIZATION
SERVICE
JULY 28, 1976

Marx

I'm not myself tonight. I don't know who I am.

—*THE COCOANUTS*

★

Lennon

Look at me.
Who am I supposed to be?
Who am I supposed to be?

—"LOOK AT ME"

Marx

Suffice it to say (which is how a lawyer of mine used to begin all his sentences—but unfortunately he had nothing to say after that. And neither have I).

—*THE GROUCHO LETTERS*

★

Lennon

I've got nothing to say but it's o.k.

—"GOOD MORNING, GOOD MORNING"
BY JOHN LENNON AND PAUL MCCARTNEY

Marx

Would you like to join me for moon-gazing some night,
when there isn't any moon?

—*THE SECRET WORD IS GROUCHO*

★

Lennon

Moonlight on the water,
Sunlight on my face,
You and me together,
We are in our place.

—"CLEANUP TIME"

Marx

Remember men, we're fighting for this woman's honor, which is probably more than she ever did.

—*Duck Soup*

★

Lennon

Don't call him "sir." He's got enough delusions of power as it is.

—*A Hard Day's Night*

Marx

I was going to thrash them within an inch of their lives,
but I didn't have a tape measure.

—*Go West*

★

Lennon

Instant Karma's gonna get you,
Gonna knock you right on the head,
You better get yourself together,
Pretty soon, you're gonna be dead.

—"Instant Karma!"

Marx

This is like living in Pittsburgh, if you call that living.

—*A Night in Casablanca*

★

Lennon

I was educated at the London School of
Depression.

—*Skywriting by Word of Mouth*

Marx

We're not very formal on the show, so do you mind if I call you Captain?

—To an Admiral
   on *You Bet Your Life*

★

Lennon

So Sgt. Pepper took you by surprise,
You better see right thru that mother's eyes.

—"How Do You Sleep?"

Marx

Why don't you just lie down until rigor mortis sets in?

—*ANIMAL CRACKERS*

★

Lennon

She said I know what it's like to be dead.
I know what it is to be sad.
And she's making me feel like I've never been born.

—"SHE SAID, SHE SAID"
BY JOHN LENNON AND PAUL McCARTNEY

Marx

No one was ever lost in bed—except maybe those foolish
young honeymooners in Omaha, and even *they* were
found within three days, and no harm done.

—*BEDS*

★

Lennon

Here in some stranger's room,
Late in the afternoon,
What am I doing here at all?
Ain't no doubt about it,
I'm losing you.

—"I'M LOSING YOU"

Marx

I've worked myself up from nothing to a state of extreme poverty.

—*Monkey Business*

★

Lennon

Who knows to what heights this man might have gone if it had not been for his vertigo?

—*Skywriting by Word of Mouth*

Marx

I've been around so long I can remember Doris Day before she was a virgin.

—A<small>TTRIBUTED</small>

Lennon

Like the F.B.I.
And the C.I.A.
And the B.B.C.
B. B. King.
And Doris Day.

—"D<small>IG</small> I<small>T</small>"
<small>BY</small> J<small>OHN</small> L<small>ENNON</small>, P<small>AUL</small> M<small>C</small>C<small>ARTNEY</small>,
G<small>EORGE</small> H<small>ARRISON</small>, <small>AND</small> R<small>INGO</small> S<small>TARR</small>

Marx

Until you have brushed a woman's cheek with your trembling lips and brushed your shoes with your wife's new guest towel, you know nothing about love—or your wife.

—*Memoirs of a Mangy Lover*

★

Lennon

You've got to run
You've got to hide
You've got to keep your woman satisfied
But it's so hard, it's really hard
Sometimes I feel like going down.

—"It's So Hard"

Marx

Have the florist send some roses to Mrs. Upjohn and write "Emily, I love you" on the back of the bill.

—A Day at the Races

Lennon

Cellophane flowers of yellow and green,
towering over your head.
Look for the girl with the sun in her eyes,
and she's gone.

—"Lucy in the Sky with Diamonds"
by John Lennon and Paul McCartney

Marx

I chased a woman for almost two years, only to discover that her tastes were exactly like mine: we both were crazy about girls.

—*The Groucho Letters*

★

Lennon

She's a big teaser,
She took me half the way there,
She was a day tripper,
One way ticket, yeah.
It took me so long to find out,
And I found out.

—"Day Tripper"
by John Lennon and Paul McCartney

Marx

Why, I'd horsewhip you if I had a horse.

—*Horse Feathers*

★

Lennon

I never forget an elephant.

—*Skywriting by Word of Mouth*

Marx

I've heard of you and you've heard of me. Now have you
ever heard the one about the two Irishmen?

—*Animal Crackers*

★

Lennon

I know you, you know me.
One thing I can tell you is you got to be free.

—"Come Together"
    by John Lennon and Paul McCartney

Marx

Room service? Send up a larger room.

—A<small>TTRIBUTED</small>

Lennon

If you can't find us a house, see if you can get us a large car.

—T<small>O</small> N<small>AT</small> W<small>EISS, WHO WAS HAVING DIFFICULTY FINDING</small> A PLACE FOR THE B<small>EATLES</small> TO STAY IN L<small>OS</small> A<small>NGELES,</small> ACCORDING TO *T<small>HE</small> B<small>ALLAD OF</small> J<small>OHN AND</small> Y<small>OKO</small>*

Marx

Why was I with her? She reminds me of you. In fact, she reminds me more of you than you do! . . . That's why I'm sitting here with you, because you remind me of you. Your eyes, your throat, your lips! Everything about you reminds me of you. Except you. How do you account for that?

—*A Night at the Opera*

★

Lennon

REPORTER: What have you seen that you like best about our country?
JOHN: You!

—Press conference
Washington, D.C.
February 11, 1964

Marx

I tried boiling pig's feet once, but I couldn't get the pig to stand still.

—To a cook
on *You Bet Your Life*

★

Lennon

See how they run like pigs from a gun,
See how they fly, I'm crying.

—"I Am the Walrus"
by John Lennon and Paul McCartney

Marx

Life is short, let's live while we may, for tomorrow the landlord may be here for the rent.

—Flywheel, Shyster, and Flywheel

★

Lennon

Life is very short
And there's no time
For fussing and fighting my friend.

—"We Can Work It Out"
by John Lennon and Paul McCartney

Marx

I'd rather have him here than in the White House.

—WHEN ASKED ABOUT HIS NEW NEIGHBOR, RICHARD NIXON,
WHO MOVED TO BEVERLY HILLS AFTER LOSING
THE 1960 PRESIDENTIAL ELECTION TO JOHN F. KENNEDY,
ACCORDING TO *THE GROUCHO PHILE*

★

Lennon

No shorthaired yellow-bellied son of Tricky Dicky
is gonna Mother Hubbard soft soap me with
just a pocketful of hope.

—"GIMME SOME TRUTH"

Marx

If you want to send ten dollars to your father you have to keep it quiet, or your wife will say you didn't marry your father—which is perfectly silly because your father is already married, and happy, too—providing you send him the ten dollars, which you probably won't—times being what they are and your father being what he is.

—Memoirs of a Mangy Lover

★

Lennon

"It's not that we don't like you dad."
Our eyes were downcast down.
"We've tried to make a go of it
Yer shriveled little clown!"

—A Spaniard in the Works

Marx

I could dance till the cows come home. On second thought, I'd rather dance with the cows till you come home.

—*DUCK SOUP*

★

Lennon

When I'm getting home tonight,
I'm gonna hold her tight,
I'm gonna love her till the cows come home,
I'll bet I'll love her more,
Till I walk out that door—again.

—"WHEN I GET HOME"
BY JOHN LENNON AND PAUL MCCARTNEY

Marx

But we learn from our mistakes. That is what
distinguishes us from the apes. (*That* and the fact that,
whereas Johnny Weissmuller is in the habit of
impersonating apes, no ape has ever found it advisable
to impersonate Johnny Weissmuller.)

—*MANY HAPPY RETURNS*

★

Lennon

"We live and learn," I told her. "Only by trying on
other people's clothes do we find what size we are."

—*SKYWRITING BY WORD OF MOUTH*

Marx

I read in the newspapers they are going to have 30
minutes of intellectual stuff on television every Monday
from 7:30 to 8 . . . to educate America. They couldn't
educate America if they started at 6:30.

—*BOSTON GLOBE*

Lennon

Keep you doped with religion and sex and TV,
And you think you're so clever and classless and free,
But you're still fucking peasants as far as I can see,
A working class hero is something to be.

—*"WORKING CLASS HERO"*

Marx

MAN: There's a man outside wants to see you with a
black moustache.
GROUCHO: Tell him I've got one.

—*THE COCOANUTS*

★

Lennon

REPORTER: How do you feel about teenagers
imitating you with Beatle wigs?
JOHN: They're not imitating us because we don't
wear Beatle wigs.

—PRESS CONFERENCE
NORTH AMERICA
1965

Marx

I'd buy you a parachute if I thought it wouldn't open.

—Animal Crackers

★

Lennon

I have found, personally, that is, that if you lean
a little backwards you're not liable to fall on your face.

—Skywriting by Word of Mouth

Marx

Many physicians recommend sleeping on the floor if you arrive home late at night half crocked. . . . I, on the other hand, advise you to forget the doctors, and advise you to sleep on the floor when sober. It has many things to recommend it. To begin with, you eliminate the cost of a bed. The money saved here can then be used for getting drunk again. Moreover, if you sleep on the floor there is no danger of falling—unless you happen to be sleeping near an open manhole.

—*GROUCHO AND ME*

★

Lennon

I'm so tired, I haven't slept a wink.
I'm so tired, my mind is on the blink.
I wonder should I get up and fix myself a drink.

—"I'M SO TIRED"
BY JOHN LENNON AND PAUL MCCARTNEY

Marx

GROUCHO: You know, I think you're the most beautiful
woman in the whole world.

WOMAN: Do you really?

GROUCHO: No, but I don't mind lying if it will get me
somewhere.

—*A NIGHT IN CASABLANCA*

Lennon

She's not a girl that misses much.

She's well acquainted with touch of the velvet
hand like a lizard on a window pane.

The man in the crowd with the multicolored
mirrors on his hobnailed boots, lying with his
eyes while his hands are busy working
overtime.

—"HAPPINESS IS A WARM GUN"
BY JOHN LENNON AND PAUL MCCARTNEY

Marx

Any woman who has the choice between a job and housework is mad if she doesn't grab the job. Man was pretty foxy to foist housework on the female. It's not that it's such hard work, but Christ, it sure is monotonous and dull. All the people you see: milkmen, garbage men, mailmen, electricians, plumbers and carpenters. In flush times, perhaps an occasional Hoover salesman, or Holeproof sock vendor. The only advantage it can possibly have for a woman is that it eliminates the necessity of wearing high heels.

—*LOVE, GROUCHO*

★

Lennon

We make her paint her face and dance,
If she won't be a slave, we say that she don't
    love us.
If she's real, we say she's trying to be a man,
While putting her down we pretend that she is
    above us.

Woman is the nigger of the world . . . yes she is
If you don't believe me take a look to the one
    you're with
Woman is the slave of the slaves
Ah yeah . . . better scream about it.

—"Woman Is the Nigger of the World"
by John Lennon and Yoko Ono

Marx

It made me laugh, scream and guffaw (which, inciden-
tally, is a great name for a law firm).

—The Groucho Letters

★

Lennon

Never underestimate the power of attorney.

—Skywriting by Word of Mouth

Marx

You're just wasting your breath and that's no great loss
either.

—MONKEY BUSINESS

Lennon

Ev'rybody's talking about
Bagism, Shagism, Dragism, Madism, Ragism,
   Tagism
This-ism, that-ism, is-m, is-m, is-m.

—"GIVE PEACE A CHANCE"
BY JOHN LENNON AND PAUL MCCARTNEY

Marx

There are many bonds that will hold us together through
eternity: your government bonds, your savings bonds,
your liberty bonds, maybe in a year or two after we're
married—who knows?—there may be a little baby bond.

—*THE BIG STORE*

★

Lennon

After all is said and done,
The two of us are really one.

—"DEAR YOKO"

Marx

A fool and his money are soon parted, but nobody can part a $2 toupee.

—*BEDS*

★

Lennon

REPORTER: They think your haircuts are
un-American.
JOHN: Well, it was very observant of them
because we aren't American, actually.

—PRESS CONFERENCE
LONDON AIRPORT
FEBRUARY 5, 1964

Marx

I've had a perfectly wonderful evening. But this wasn't it.

—ATTRIBUTED

★

Lennon

Life is what happens to you while you're busy making other plans.

—"BEAUTIFUL BOY (DARLING BOY)"

Marx

I have nothing but confidence in you. And very little of that.

—In *As Long As They're Laughing*
   by Robert Dwan

★

Lennon

You'll never know how much I appreciate your
kindness unless, of course, you ask.

—*Skywriting by Word of Mouth*

Marx

Your first impulse is to run upstairs and get your
revolver, then you suddenly remember that the revolver
wouldn't be much good, for you hid the bullets so that
the kids wouldn't murder one another.

—*Memoirs of a Mangy Lover*

★

Lennon

Whatever gets you to the light—'salright, 'salright.
Out the blue or out of sight—'salright, 'salright.
Don't need a gun to blow your mind—oh no, oh no.

—"Whatever Gets You Thru the Night"

Marx

Some people claim that marriage interferes with romance. There's no doubt about it. Anytime you have a romance, your wife is bound to interfere.

—*THE GROUCHO PHILE*

★

Lennon

Somebody needs to know the time,
Glad that I'm here.
Watching the skirts you start to flirt,
Now you're in gear.

—"GOOD MORNING, GOOD MORNING"
BY JOHN LENNON AND PAUL McCARTNEY

Marx

Africa is God's country and He can have it.

—*ANIMAL CRACKERS*

★

Lennon

Possession is nine-tenths of the problem.

—LINER NOTES
WALLS AND BRIDGES

Marx

Why, a four-year-old child could understand this report.
Run out and find me a four-year-old child. I can't make
head or tail out of it.

—*DUCK SOUP*

★

Lennon

Don't worry, son, we'll get you the best lawyer
trading stamps can buy.

—*A HARD DAY'S NIGHT*

Marx

Why don't you go home to your wife? I tell you what. I'll go home to your wife and, outside of the improvement, she'll never know the difference.

—*Horse Feathers*

★

Lennon

He'd tried wife-swapping, but mother-swapping was something else.

—*Skywriting by Word of Mouth*

Marx

I can't hide it any longer. I love you. It's the old story, boy meets girl—Romeo and Juliet—Minneapolis and St. Paul.

—*A Day at the Races*

★

Lennon

'Cause I'm the fish and you're the sea.
'Cause I'm the apple and you're the tree.
'Cause I'm the door and you're the key.
'Cause I'm the honey and you're the bee.

—"One Day (at a Time)"

Marx

She got her looks from her father. He's a plastic surgeon.

—ATTRIBUTED

★

Lennon

Although I laugh and act like a clown,
Beneath this mask I am wearing a frown.

—"I'M A LOSER"
BY JOHN LENNON AND PAUL MCCARTNEY

Marx

When I invite a woman to dinner, I expect her to look at
my face. That's the price she has to pay.

—A Night at the Opera

★

Lennon

If a psychic doesn't know what time he's coming
to dinner, how the hell am I supposed to know?

—Skywriting by Word of Mouth

Marx

Money will never make you happy, and happy will never make you money.

—*The Cocoanuts*

★

Lennon

I don't care too much for money,
Money can't buy me love.

—"Can't Buy Me Love"
by John Lennon and Paul McCartney

Marx

The weather became as mild as a review in a trade paper after you've taken an ad.

—*THE GROUCHO LETTERS*

★

Lennon

Tomorrow will be Muggy, followed by Tuggy, Wuggy, and Thuggy.

—*THE DAILY HOWL*

Marx

Most young women do not welcome promiscuous
advances. (Either that, or my luck's been terrible.)

—*Memoirs of a Mangy Lover*

★

Lennon

But if you go carrying pictures of Chairman Mao,
You ain't gonna make it with anyone anyhow.

—"Revolution"
by John Lennon and Paul McCartney

Marx

Beads of perspiration started on my forehead and trickled down my face to my neck, forming a rather unbecoming bead necklace.

—"How to Build a Secret Weapon"

★

Lennon

A flood of memories drowned him in a pool of sweat.

—*Skywriting by Word of Mouth*

Marx

I wish you'd keep my hands to yourself.

—*MONKEY BUSINESS*

★

Lennon

We're all alone and there's nobody else,
You still moan, "Keep your hands to yourself."

—"I'M DOWN"
BY JOHN LENNON AND PAUL MCCARTNEY

Marx

And remember while you're out there risking life and
limb through shot and shell, we'll be in here thinking
what a sucker you are.

—*Duck Soup*

★

Lennon

Well, I don't wanna be a lawyer mama, I don't
    wanna lie.
Well, I don't wanna be a soldier mama, I don't
    wanna die.

—"I Don't Wanna Be a Soldier Mama,
    I Don't Wanna Die"

Marx

The nickel today is not what it was fifteen years ago. Do you know what this country needs today? . . . A seven-cent nickel. Yessiree, we've been using the five-cent nickel in this country since 1492. Now that's pretty near a hundred years daylight saving. Now, why not give the seven-cent nickel a chance? If that works out, next year we could have an eight-cent nickel. Think what that would mean. You could go to a newsstand, buy a three-cent newspaper and get the same nickel back again. One nickel carefully used would last a family a lifetime!

—*Animal Crackers*

Lennon

For only $10 a day you can have a picture of a penthouse, still live in a ghetto, and pretend you're living in a luxury apartment!!! SEND $40. LIVE LIKE A KING. Offer expires every thirty minutes.

—*Skywriting by Word of Mouth*

Marx

GROUCHO: What does a girl think when she meets a handsome boy?

GIRL: Oh, I imagine she thinks about the same things boys do.

GROUCHO: You mean girls too wonder if they'll be drafted?

—*YOU BET YOUR LIFE*

Lennon

REPORTER: Where do you gentlemen stand as far as the draft is concerned in England?

JOHN: About five eleven.

—PRESS CONFERENCE
INDIANAPOLIS, INDIANA
SEPTEMBER 3, 1964

Marx

A black cat crossing your path signifies that the animal
is going somewhere.

—Attributed

★

Lennon

Well you know that your cat has nine lives babe,
Nine lives to itself,
But you only got one and a dog's life ain't fun,
Mama take a look outside.

—"Crippled Inside"

Marx

We will be just in time to be fashionably late.

—*LOVE HAPPY*

★

Lennon

Don't need a watch to waste your time—oh no, oh no.

—"WHATEVER GETS YOU THRU THE NIGHT"

Marx

Hello, I must be going,
I cannot stay,
I came to say,
I must be going.
I'm glad I came,
But just the same,
I must be going.

—"HOORAY FOR CAPTAIN SPAULDING"
BY BERT KALMAR AND HARRY RUBY

★

Lennon

You say yes,

I say no,

You say stop,

And I say go, go, go.

I don't know why you say goodbye,

I say hello.

You say goodbye,

And I say hello.

—"Hello, Goodbye"
by John Lennon and Paul McCartney

Marx

On my opening night in "Twentieth Century" the audience cheered for twenty minutes at the end of the first act, but for some reason or other never returned for the next two acts.

—"That Marx Guy Again"

★

Lennon

REPORTER: Can we look forward to any more
    Beatle movies?
JOHN: Well, there'll be many more but I don't
    know whether you can look forward to them
    or not.

—Press conference
New York
August 23, 1966

Marx

Why don't you bore a hole in yourself and let the sap
run out?

—*HORSE FEATHERS*

★

Lennon

Who in the hell d'you think you are?
A super star?
Well, right you are.

—"INSTANT KARMA!"

Marx

Many people get a good night's rest by counting sheep. If possible, it's advisable to have the sheep in the bedroom. However, if you are allergic to wool (and most of the woolen sweaters I buy seem to be), you can also court sleep by counting panthers. Of course, there is always the danger that the panthers may eat you, but if you suffer from insomnia that is really the best thing that can happen to you.

—*Groucho and Me*

★

Lennon

Insomnia was cured by putting people to sleep.

—*Skywriting by Word of Mouth*

Marx

Well, the chances are you are lying in your teeth, if they *are* your teeth.

—*MANY HAPPY RETURNS*

★

Lennon

I'm sick and tired of hearing things
From uptight short-sighted narrow-minded
    hypocritics
All I want is the truth.
Just gimme some truth.

—"GIMME SOME TRUTH"

Marx

I will be home in another ten days and will reveal many
things that will make your hair stand on end—assuming
that you still have any.

—*THE GROUCHO LETTERS*

★

Lennon

I got a whole lot of things to tell her,
    when I get home.
Come on, I'm on my way,
'Cause I'm gonna see my baby today,
I've got a whole lot of things I gotta say to her.

—"WHEN I GET HOME"
BY JOHN LENNON AND PAUL MCCARTNEY

Marx

WOMAN: I am half Italian, half French.

GROUCHO: Well, that's a nice combination—half French, half Italian. You oughta have a lot of happy thoughts. I know a fellow who's half Scotch and half Soda, and he's happy all the time.

—*YOU BET YOUR LIFE*

★

Lennon

If you had the luck of the Irish,
You'd be sorry and wish you were dead.
You should have the luck of the Irish,
And you'd wish you was English instead.

—"LUCK OF THE IRISH"
BY JOHN LENNON AND YOKO ONO

Marx

The country needs men's hats that can be neatly folded
and put away in your pocket so you won't have to buy
them back from the hatcheck girl.

—"WHAT THIS COUNTRY NEEDS"

★

Lennon

At the drop of a hatcheck girl he would give forth
on various subjects, ranging from the ridiculous
to Mamie Eisenhower.

—*SKYWRITING BY WORD OF MOUTH*

Marx

You mind if I don't smoke?

—*ANIMAL CRACKERS*

★

Lennon

Expert texpert, choking smokers, don't you think
the joker laughs at you?

—"I AM THE WALRUS"
BY JOHN LENNON AND PAUL MCCARTNEY

Marx

Now then, I've got an idea so brilliant that it doesn't seem possible that I thought it up.

—*Memoirs of a Mangy Lover*

★

Lennon

PLAYBOY: *Did* you put aeolian cadences in "It Won't Be Long"?

JOHN: To this day I don't have *any* idea what they are. They sound like exotic birds.

—*The Playboy Interviews with John Lennon and Yoko Ono*

Marx

WOMAN: My husband is dead.

GROUCHO: I'll bet he's just using that as an excuse.

WOMAN: I was with him to the end.

GROUCHO: No wonder he passed away.

WOMAN: I held him in my arms and kissed him.

GROUCHO: So it was murder.

—*DUCK SOUP*

★

Lennon

When I hold you in my arms,
And I feel my finger on your trigger,
I know no one can do me no harm,
Because happiness is a warm gun.

—"HAPPINESS IS A WARM GUN"
BY JOHN LENNON AND PAUL McCARTNEY

Marx

My boy, I think you've got something there, and I'll wait
outside until you clean it up.

—*Monkey Business*

★

Lennon

I tried water divining, it only led me to the
bathroom.

—*Skywriting by Word of Mouth*

Marx

Listen, when I want a lesson in geography, I'll speak to
Rand McNally.

—*You Bet Your Life*

Lennon

REPORTER: How did you find America?
JOHN: Turn left at Greenland.

—*A Hard Day's Night*

Marx

I have found that I can be put to sleep by (1) a fifth
cocktail; (b) a Mickey Finn, which is known in the night
clubs as a Mickey Finn; (27) radio tenors who songfully
yearn for Alabamy and want to go there as much as I want
to go back to the reform school; (x) a letter from Aunt
Susie; (164) Henry James' later novels—I never opened
the earlier ones; (c) a Bach concerto, although Bach beer
makes me even drowsier; (pdq) business forecasts by in-
dustrial giants who tell us conditions are great, but that
we shouldn't worry anyway; (tw) a half-hour of Clara
Bow's chemise (I mean on the screen), which gives you
an idea how my youth is slipping (he slipped on his way
to school yesterday, and I warned him to be more careful);
(s) speeches by Mussolini; (97) speeches by anybody; a
light sock on the jaw; (29) yo yo tops—and a bottle of rum.

—*BEDS*

★

Lennon

A   is for Parrot which we can plainly see
B   is for glasses which we can plainly see
C   is for plastic which we can plainly see
D   is for Doris
E   is for binoculars I'll get it in five
F   is for Ethel who lives next door
G   is for orange which we love to eat when we can
      get them because they come from abroad
H   is for England and (Heather)
I   is for monkey we see in the tree
J   is for parrot which we can plainly see
K   is for shoetop we wear to the ball
L   is for Land because brown
M   is for Venezuela where the oranges come from
N   is for Brazil near Venezuela (very near)
O   is for football which we kick about a bit
T   is for Tommy who won the war

Q	is for garden which we can plainly see
R	is for intestines which hurt when we dance
S	is for pancake or whole wheat bread
U	is for Ethel who lives on the hill
P	is arab and her sister will
V	is for me
W	is for lighter which never lights
X	is for easter—have one yourself
Y	is a crooked letter and you can't straighten it
Z	is for apple which we can plainly see

This is my story both humble and true
Take it to pieces and mend it with glue

—"AN ALPHABET," FEBRUARY 1969

Marx

I wish to be cremated. One-tenth of my ashes shall be given to my agent.

—ATTRIBUTED

★

Lennon

Nobody loves you when you're old and grey
Nobody needs you when you're upside down
Everybody's hollerin' 'bout their own birthday
Everybody loves you when you're six foot in the
     ground.

—"NOBODY LOVES YOU (WHEN YOU'RE DOWN AND OUT)"

Marx

Don't go away and leave me here alone. You stay here and I'll go away.

—*THE COCOANUTS*

★

Lennon

I leave you as I found you—only some time later.

—*SKYWRITING BY WORD OF MOUTH*

Marx

I eat like a vulture. Unfortunately, the resemblance
doesn't end there.

—*THE GROUCHO LETTERS*

★

Lennon

I too play the guitar. Sometimes I play the fool.

—*THE PUBLIC EAR*
BBC, NOVEMBER 3, 1963

Marx

WOMAN: Sir, what can I do for you?

GROUCHO: Madam, we'll discuss that later. Right now my mind is on business.

—*BEAGLE, SHYSTER, AND BEAGLE*

★

Lennon

REPORTER: Was your family in show business?

JOHN: Well, me dad used to say me mother was a great performer.

—PRESS CONFERENCE
NEW YORK'S KENNEDY AIRPORT
FEBRUARY 7, 1964

Marx

WOMAN: Will you join me?
GROUCHO: Why? Are you coming apart?

—*A Night in Casablanca*

★

Lennon

Suddenly, I'm not half the man I used to be,
'Cause now I'm an amputee.

—"Yesterday (Parody)"

Marx

There's a girl out there with a loose sweater. I wish there
was a loose girl out there with a tight sweater. I'd
certainly like to pull the wool over *her* eyes.

—*The Secret Word Is Groucho*

★

Lennon

Dear Prudence, won't you come out to play?
Dear Prudence, greet the brand new day.
The sun is up, the sky is blue,
It's beautiful and so are you.
Dear Prudence, won't you come out to play?

—"Dear Prudence"
by John Lennon and Paul McCartney

Marx

Oh, I love sitting on your lap. I could sit here all day if
you didn't stand up.

—Horse Feathers

Lennon

So we'll settle down, deeply, I hope, and comfort-
ably in an easy chair.

—"The Great Wok"

Marx

It's pretty hard to be wrong if you keep answering
yourself all the time.

—*Animal Crackers*

★

Lennon

I can prove it beyond a shadow of a doubting
Thomas.

—*Skywriting by Word of Mouth*

Marx

I believe that wives have a definite place in the home.
They're invaluable as mothers, and also for keeping you
informed as to when the lady next door gets a new car, a
new fur stole, or is taken out dancing.

—*MEMOIRS OF A MANGY LOVER*

★

Lennon

Everyone you see is full of life.
It's time for tea and meet the wife.

—"GOOD MORNING, GOOD MORNING"
BY JOHN LENNON AND PAUL MCCARTNEY

Marx

She was headstrong and footstrong too.

—*I'll Say She Is!*

★

Lennon

YOKO: Fortunately, we both agree.
JOHN: Unfortunately, not always.

—"Fortunately"

Marx

You call this a party? The beer is warm, the women are cold, and I'm hot under the collar.

—*MONKEY BUSINESS*

★

Lennon

I don't want to spoil the party so I'll go,
I would hate my disappointment to show,
There's nothing for me here,
So I will disappear,
If she turns up while I'm gone please let me
    know.

—"I DON'T WANT TO SPOIL THE PARTY"
BY JOHN LENNON AND PAUL MCCARTNEY

Marx

Who are you going to believe, me or those crooked
X-rays?

—*A Day at the Races*

★

Lennon

Reality leaves a lot to the imagination.

—*The Way It Is*
CBC-TV, June 8, 1969

Marx

I can see you right now in the kitchen bending over a hot stove . . . but I can't see the stove.

—*DUCK SOUP*

★

Lennon

There's always something cooking and nothing
    in the pot.
They're starving back in China so finish what
    you got.

—"NOBODY TOLD ME"

Marx

He is the only man I know who can take a beautiful love song, send it through his nose and have it come out sounding like an air raid warning.

—*The Groucho Letters*

★

Lennon

There's nothing you can do that can't be done,
Nothing you can sing that can't be sung.

—"All You Need Is Love"
by John Lennon and Paul McCartney

Marx

WOMAN: I'm afraid after we're married awhile, a beautiful
    girl will come along and you'll forget all about me.
GROUCHO: Don't be silly. I'll write you twice a week.

    —*THE BIG STORE*

★

Lennon

    When I think of all the times
        I tried so hard to leave her,
    She will turn to me and start to cry,
    And she promises the earth to me
        and I believe her,
    After all this time I don't know why.

      —"GIRL"
        BY JOHN LENNON AND PAUL MCCARTNEY

Marx

Now I know why you travel so much.

—To Eleanor Roosevelt,
after hearing the Marine band at the White House,
according to *The Groucho Phile*

★

Lennon

REPORTER: Where would you like to go that you
haven't gone yet?
JOHN: Home.

—Press conference
Chicago, Illinois
September 5, 1964

Marx

I'm going to see that you get a steady position. And if I can arrange it, it will be horizontal.

—*THE COCOANUTS*

Lennon

She asked me to stay
   and she told me to sit anywhere,
But I looked around
   and I noticed there wasn't a chair.

—"NORWEGIAN WOOD"
BY JOHN LENNON AND PAUL MCCARTNEY

Marx

The first morning saw us up at six, breakfasted, and
back in bed at seven. This was our routine for the first
three months. We finally got so we were back in bed at
six thirty.

—*ANIMAL CRACKERS*

★

Lennon

The foreseeable future looked terrifying, so I
took to walking backwards.

—*SKYWRITING BY WORD OF MOUTH*

Marx

Quote me as saying I was misquoted.

—ATTRIBUTED

★

Lennon

Everybody's talking and no one says a word.

—"NOBODY TOLD ME"

Marx

You claim you own *Casablanca* and that no one else can use that name without your permission. What about "Warner Brothers"? Do you own that, too? You probably have the right to use the word Warner, but what about Brothers? Professionally, we were brothers long before you were.

—LETTER TO WARNER BROTHERS, WHO HAD THREATENED TO TAKE LEGAL ACTION IF THE MARX BROTHERS TITLED THEIR NEXT MOVIE *A NIGHT IN CASABLANCA,* IN *THE GROUCHO LETTERS*

★

Lennon

Many people ask what are the Beatles? Why Beatles? Ugh, Beatles how did the name arrive? So we will tell you. It came in a vision—a man appeared on a flaming pie and said unto them "From this day on you are Beatles with an A." Thank you, Mister Man, they said, thanking him.

—"BEING A SHORT DIVERSION ON THE DUBIOUS ORIGINS OF BEATLES"

Marx

Gentlemen?

If you continue to write nasty pieces about me, I shall be obliged to cancel my subscription.

—Letter to the editor of *Confidential Magazine*,
in *Groucho and Me*

★

Lennon

If it don't feel right, don't do it.
Just leave a message on the phone and tell them
to screw it.

—"I'm Stepping Out"

Marx

Well, that covers a lot of ground. Say, you cover a lot of ground yourself. You'd better beat it. I hear they're going to tear you down and put an office building where you're standing.

—*Duck Soup*

★

Lennon

She was losing ground at $160 an acre.

—*Skywriting by Word of Mouth*

Marx

GROUCHO: Call me Montgomery.

WOMAN: Is that your name?

GROUCHO: No, I'm just breaking it in for a friend.

—*A Night in Casablanca*

★

Lennon

Yes, my name is Billy Shears,
You know it has been for so many years,
Now I'm only thirty-two,
And all I want to do is boogaloo.

—"I'm the Greatest"

Marx

Do I plan to play Hamlet? No, we couldn't think of playing any town under a hundred thousand—not with road conditions as they are.

—"Bad Days Are Good Memories"

★

Lennon

PLAYBOY: OK, we're on. Why don't we begin by . . .

JOHN: Doing Hamlet.

—Interview by Jean Shepherd
Playboy
February 1965

Marx

You know how to make a Venetian blind? Get him drunk.
That's the best way.

—*YOU BET YOUR LIFE*

Lennon

He's as blind as he can be,
Just sees what he wants to see,
Nowhere Man can you see me at all?

—"NOWHERE MAN"
BY JOHN LENNON AND PAUL MCCARTNEY

Marx

Now, suppose your feet grew in the shape of wheels?
You'd really have something then. You could roll around
and see your friends, you could roll to the vegetable
market, and in the evening when you came home from
work, your wife could tie a suction bag around your neck
and use you for a vacuum cleaner.

—"Groucho Marx Turns Himself In For Scrap"

★

Lennon

I'm just sitting here watching the wheels go
   round and round,
I really love to watch them roll,
No longer riding on the merry-go-round,
I just had to let it go.

—"Watching the Wheels"

Marx

I don't want anything elaborate. Just a little place that I can call home and tell the wife I won't be there for dinner.

—*Animal Crackers*

★

Lennon

Next week we'll discuss "How to Satisfy a Dead Housewife," a closer look at feminism by the author of "Take My Wife Anywhere" . . .

—*Skywriting by Word of Mouth*

Marx

I know it's often been said that money won't make you happy and this is undeniably true, but everything else being equal, it's a lovely thing to have around the house.

—*Memoirs of a Mangy Lover*

★

Lennon

Baby you're a rich man,
Baby you're a rich man,
Baby you're a rich man too.
You keep all your money in a big brown bag
　　inside a zoo.
What a thing to do.

—"Baby You're a Rich Man"
by John Lennon and Paul McCartney

Marx

The secret of success is honesty and fair dealing. If you can fake those, you've got it made.

—Attributed

Lennon

REPORTER: What is the secret of your success?
JOHN: We have a press agent.

—Press conference
New York's Kennedy Airport
February 7, 1964

Marx

My plans are still in embryo. In case you've never been there, this is a small town on the outskirts of wishful thinking.

—*THE GROUCHO LETTERS*

★

Lennon

All my little plans and schemes,
Gone like some forgotten dream.

—"REAL LOVE"

Marx

I'll meet you tonight under the moon. Oh, I can see you now. You and the moon. You wear a necktie so I'll know you.

—*THE COCOANUTS*

★

Lennon

Picture yourself on a train in a station,
With plasticine porters with looking glass ties,
Suddenly someone is there at the turnstile,
The girl with kaleidoscope eyes.

—"LUCY IN THE SKY WITH DIAMONDS"
BY JOHN LENNON AND PAUL MCCARTNEY

Marx

You have my word, and you know what that's worth.

—*ROOM SERVICE*

★

Lennon

Say the word and you'll be free,
Say the word and be like me,
Say the word I'm thinking of,
Have you heard the word is love.

—"THE WORD"
BY JOHN LENNON AND PAUL McCARTNEY

Marx

You know the old saying. An ounce of prevention is
worth a pound of bandages and adhesive tape.

—*You Bet Your Life*

★

Lennon

Madness is the first sign of dandruff.

—Liner notes
Mind Games

Marx

I'm a man of one word: scram!

—*Duck Soup*

★

Lennon

But let us begin somewhere in the middle of
nowhere in particular, for that was exactly where
he found himself, or should I say lost himself?
Or should I say get lost?

—*Skywriting by Word of Mouth*

Marx

Mad with excitement I flung up my hands. One hit the ceiling and the other landed in a wastebasket.

—"How to Build a Secret Weapon"

★

Lennon

It was little Bobby's birthmark today and he got a surprise. His very fist was lopped off, (The War) and he got a birthday hook!

All his life Bobby had wanted his very own hook; and now on his 39th birthday his pwayers had been answered. The only trouble was they had send him a left hook and ebry dobby knows that it was Bobby's right fist that was missing as it were.

What to do was not thee only problem: Anyway he jopped off his lest hand and it fitted like a glove. Maybe next year he will get a right hook, who knows?

—*In His Own Write*

Marx

As the Chinese poet, Ah Ling, put it (in the waste-basket):

> The more the moolah
> You make in your racket,
> The quicker you go
> In a higher bracket.

—*MANY HAPPY RETURNS*

★

Lennon

Now let me tell you, my resolution for the year 1979 is to renounce complete everything, but complete luxury and self-indulgence.

—"THE GREAT WOK"

Marx

It isn't politics that makes strange bedfellows. It's matrimony.

—*BEDS*

★

Lennon

Drove from Paris to the Amsterdam Hilton,
Talking in our beds for a week,
The newspapers said,
Say what're you doing in bed,
I said we're only trying to get us some peace.

—"THE BALLAD OF JOHN AND YOKO"
BY JOHN LENNON AND PAUL MCCARTNEY

Marx

Why, you've got beauty, charm, money. You have got
money, haven't you? 'Cause if you haven't, we can quit
right now.

—*ANIMAL CRACKERS*

★

Lennon

REPORTER: If you were not singers, what would
   you like to be?
JOHN: Just rich, I think.

—PRESS CONFERENCE
SAN FRANCISCO, CALIFORNIA
AUGUST 31, 1965

Marx

Do you suppose I could buy back my introduction to you?

—*MONKEY BUSINESS*

★

Lennon

Did you get my last letter or did it go over your
head?

—*SKYWRITING BY WORD OF MOUTH*

Marx

GIRL: I would say it's what's upstairs that counts.

GROUCHO: Well, I have something upstairs. My upstairs maid. And that's not easy because I only have a one-story house. And the one story you're not going to hear is about my upstairs maid.

—You Bet Your Life

★

Lennon

Lovely Rita, meter maid,
Where would I be without you?
Give us a wink and make me think of you.

—"Lovely Rita"
by John Lennon and Paul McCartney

Marx

Outside of a dog, a book is man's best friend. Inside of a
dog, it's too dark to read.

Lennon

Arf, Arf, he goes, a merry sight,
Our little hairy friend,
Arf, Arf, upon the lamppost bright
Arfing round the bend.
Nice dog! Goo boy,
Waggie tail and beg,
Clever Nigel, jump for joy
Because we're putting you to sleep at three of
    the clock, Nigel.

—In His Own Write

Marx

The neck would be much more useful if it were equipped
with ball bearings. This would enable the head to swing
completely around on its axis and, if necessary,
eventually return to its original position.

  —MEMOIRS OF A MANGY LOVER

★

Lennon

You say you'll change the constitution,
Well, you know, we all want to change your head.
You tell me it's the institution,
Well, you know, you better free your mind
  instead.

   —"REVOLUTION"
   BY JOHN LENNON AND PAUL MCCARTNEY

Marx

That reminds me of a story that's so dirty I'm ashamed to think of it myself.

—Horse Feathers

Lennon

Well now to err is something human and
    forgiving so divine,
I'll forgive your trespasses, if you forgive me
    mine.

—"Move Over Ms. L"

Marx

I wouldn't know what to say either if I was in your place.
Maybe you can suggest something. As a matter of fact,
you do suggest something. To me you suggest a baboon.

—*Duck Soup*

★

Lennon

Everybody's got something to hide except for me
and my monkey.

—Song title
by John Lennon and Paul McCartney

Marx

I'm a man and you're a woman. I can't think of a better
arrangement.

—*A Night in Casablanca*

Lennon

You are my woman,
I am your man,
Nothing else matters at all,
Now I understand.

—"One Day (At a Time)"

Marx

You're a woman who's been getting nothing but dirty breaks. Well, we can clean and tighten your brakes, but you'll have to stay in the garage all night.

—MONKEY BUSINESS

★

Lennon

Baby, you can drive my car,
Yes, I'm gonna be a star,
Baby, you can drive my car,
And maybe I'll love you.
Beep beep, beep beep, yeah!

—"DRIVE MY CAR"
BY JOHN LENNON AND PAUL MCCARTNEY

Marx

I had to leave school in the seventh grade—nobody, after all, should stay in school after the age of twenty-two.

—*THE GROUCHO PHILE*

★

Lennon

I went to finishing school in Paris but never finished.

—*SKYWRITING BY WORD OF MOUTH*

Marx

On this site we're going to build an Eye and Ear
Hospital. This is going to be a sight for sore eyes.

—*THE COCOANUTS*

★

Lennon

Oh my love for the first time in my life,
My eyes are wide open.
Oh my lover for the first time in my life,
My eyes can see.

—"OH MY LOVE"
BY JOHN LENNON AND YOKO ONO

Marx

Why should I care about posterity? What's posterity ever
done for me?

—ATTRIBUTED

Lennon

Eternity is a hell of a long time.

—*SKYWRITING BY WORD OF MOUTH*

Marx

I've got a good mind to join a club and beat you over the head with it.

—*Duck Soup*

★

Lennon

Say you're looking for some peace and love,
Leader of a big old band.
You wanna save humanity,
But it's people that you just can't stand.

—"I Don't Wanna Face It"

Marx

After that, in swift succession, we were employed by
the American Oil Company and Kellogg's Cornflakes.
If you're hungry some morning, you might try this
combination.

—GROUCHO AND ME

★

Lennon

Sitting on a cornflake waiting for the van to
    come.
Corporation t-shirt, stupid bloody Tuesday,
Man you've been a naughty boy, you let your
    face grow long.

—"I AM THE WALRUS"
BY JOHN LENNON AND PAUL MCCARTNEY

Marx

My best to you and your very sexy wife, and if she ever leaves you—I'm in the book.

—*The Groucho Letters*

★

Lennon

Sexy Sadie, what have you done?
You made a fool of everyone.

—"Sexy Sadie"
by John Lennon and Paul McCartney

Marx

Anyway I haven't been to Seattle since I appeared there at the Orpheum Theatre some twenty years ago and I am going over to the theatre and see if the same audience is sitting there.

—*Love, Groucho*

★

Lennon

I'd like to say thank you on behalf of the group and ourselves. I hope we passed the audition.

—*Let It Be*

Acknowledgments

I AM PROFOUNDLY GRATEFUL TO Yoko Ono and Arthur Marx for their enthusiasm for this book, Jonas Herbsman and Robert Finkelstein for their wise counsel, Miriam Marx Allen for her kindness, and my agent, Jeremy Solomon, for his sage advice. At Hyperion, I am deeply indebted to my editor Gretchen Young, editor-in-chief Will Schwalbe, and president Bob Miller for championing my cause and for making this book a labor of love. My heartfelt thanks to the astounding talents of cover designer Phil Rose, book designer Richard Oriolo, copyeditor Joshua Cohen, associate editor Zareen Jaffery, and editorial assistant Ruth Curry. I also thank Debbie Green for her excellent research work, Mark

Blechman for introducing me in high school to the comedy of Firesign Theatre, and Laura Strauss, Ken Krainman, Howard Gershen, Cecilia Rasmussen, Demian Caponi, and Jeffrey Combs for their guidance. I am also grateful to Christy Ikner at Sony/ATV Music Publishing, Shannon Fifer at Warner Brothers Entertainment, Veronika Beltran and Cindy Chang at Universal Studios, Karen Magid and Kevin Sheridan at Paramount Pictures, David Olsen at Warner Bros. Publications, LeeAnn Platner at NBC Studios, Barbara Slavin at *Rolling Stone,* David Schmit and Marcia Terrones at Playboy Enterprises, Colleen Aylward at *Variety,* Greg Jones at Perseus Books, Sue Svehla at Midnight Marquee Press, and Heather Marsh-Rumion at Corbis. Above all, all my love to Debbie, Ashley, and Julia.

Bibliography

GROUCHO MARX

As Long As They're Laughing: Groucho Marx and You Bet Your Life by Robert Dwan (Baltimore, Maryland: Midnight Marquee Press, 2000).

"Bad Days Are Good Memories" by Groucho Marx, *The Saturday Evening Post,* August 29, 1931.

Beds by Groucho Marx (Indianapolis, Indiana: Bobbs-Merrill, 1976).

The Essential Groucho by Stefan Kanfer (New York: Vintage, 2000).

Flywheel, Shyster, and Flywheel: The Marx Brothers' Lost Radio Show, edited by Michael Barson (New York: Pantheon, 1988).

Groucho: A Life in Revue by Arthur Marx (New York: Samuel French, 1988).

Groucho: The Life and Times of Julius Henry Marx by Stefan Kanfer (New York: Knopf, 2000).

Groucho and Me by Groucho Marx (New York: Bernard Geis Associates, 1959).

The Groucho Letters: Letters From and To Groucho Marx by Groucho Marx (New York: Simon & Schuster, 1967).

Groucho Marx and Other Short Stories and Tall Tales, edited by Robert Bader (Boston: Faber and Faber, 1993).

The Groucho Phile: An Illustrated Life by Groucho Marx (Indianapolis: Bobbs-Merrill Company, Inc., 1976).

It's in the Book, Bob! by Bob Eubanks with Matthew Scott Hansen (Dallas, Texas: BenBella Books, 2004).

Love, Groucho: Letters from Groucho Marx to His Daughter Miriam by Groucho Marx, edited by Miriam Marx Allen (Boston: Faber and Faber, 1992).

Many Happy Returns by Groucho Marx (New York: Simon & Schuster, 1942).

The Marx Bros. Scrapbook by Groucho Marx and Richard J. Anobile (New York: Darien House, 1973).

Memoirs of a Mangy Lover by Groucho Marx (New York: Bernard Geis Associates, 1963).

Monkey Business: The Lives and Legends of the Marx Brothers by Simon Louvish (New York: St. Martin's Press, 1999).

"My Acid Trip with Groucho" by Paul Krassner, *High Times,* February 1981.

My Life with Groucho by Arthur Marx (London: Robson, 1988).

People I Have Loved, Known, or Admired by Leo Rosten (New York: McGraw-Hill, 1970).

The Secret Word Is Groucho by Groucho Marx with Hector Arce (New York: G. P. Putnam's Sons, 1976).

"The Secret Word on Groucho" by Jon Wiener, *The Nation,* September 28, 1998.

JOHN LENNON

The Ballad of John and Yoko by the editors of *Rolling Stone,* edited by Jonathan Cott and Christine Doudna (New York: Doubleday, 1982).

The Beatles Anthology by the Beatles (San Francisco: Chronicle, 2000).

The Beatles Forever by Nicholas Schaffner (New York: McGraw-Hill, 1977).

The Beatles Illustrated Lyrics, edited by Alan Aldridge (London: MacDonald, 1971).

The Gay Liberation Book, edited by Len Richmond and Gary Noguera (San Francisco: Ramparts, 1973).

Gimme Some Truth: The John Lennon FBI Files by Jon Wiener (University of California Press, 1999).

Imagine John Lennon, written and edited by Andrew Solt and Sam Egan (New York: Macmillan, 1988).

In His Own Write by John Lennon (New York: Simon & Schuster, 1964).

Lennon by Ray Coleman (New York: McGraw-Hill, 1984).

Lennon: His Life and Work, edited by James Henke (Cleveland, Ohio: The Rock and Roll Hall of Fame and Museum, 2000).

Lennon Remembers: The Rolling Stone Interviews by Jann Wenner (New York: Popular Library, 1971).

"Playboy Interview With the Beatles" conducted by Jean Shepherd in Edinburgh, *Playboy,* February 1965.

The Playboy Interviews with John Lennon and Yoko Ono, conducted by David Sheff, edited by G. Barry Golson (New York: Playboy Press, 1981).

Shout! The Beatles in Their Generation by Philip Norman (New York: Warner, 1981).

Skywriting by Word of Mouth by John Lennon (New York: HarperPerennial, 1986).

A Spaniard in the Works by John Lennon (New York: Simon & Schuster, 1965).

Strawberry Fields Forever: John Lennon Remembered by Vic Garbarini and Brian Cullman with Barbara Graustark (New York: Bantam, 1980).

Ticket to Ride by Larry Kane (Philadelphia: Running Press, 2003).

Copyright Information

The quotes throughout this book were taken from the following sources:

GROUCHO MARX

Movie Dialogue

Animal Crackers, screenplay by Morrie Ryskind, based on the musical play by George S. Kaufman, Bert Kalmar, Morrie Ryskind, and Harry Ruby. Copyright © 1930 Paramount Publix Corporation. Renewed 1957 Paramount Pictures Corporation. All rights reserved. Used with permission.

At the Circus, screenplay by Irving Brecher. Copyright © 1939 Turner Entertainment Company. All rights reserved. Used with permission.

The Big Store, screenplay by Sid Kuller, Hal Fimberg, and Ray

Golden; original story by Nat Pierria, MGM. Copyright © 1941 Turner Entertainment Company. All rights reserved. Used with permission.

The Cocoanuts, based on the play and book by George S. Kaufman and Morrie Ryskind, screen adaptation by Morrie Ryskind. Copyright © 1929 Paramount Famous Lasky Corp. Renewed 1956 Paramount Pictures Corporation. All rights reserved. Used with permission.

A Day at the Races, script by Robert Pirosh, George Seaton, and George Oppenheimer. Copyright © 1937 Turner Entertainment Company. All rights reserved. Used with permission.

Duck Soup, screenplay by Bert Kalmar and Harry Ruby, additional dialogue by Arthur Sheekman and Nat Perrin. Copyright © 1933 Paramount Productions, Inc. Renewed 1960 by EMKA, Ltd. All rights reserved. Used with permission.

Go West, screenplay by Irving Brecher. Copyright © 1940 Turner Entertainment Company. All rights reserved. Used with permission.

Horse Feathers, screenplay by Burt Kalmar, Harry Ruby, and S. J. Perelman. Copyright © 1932 Paramount Publix Corp. Renewed 1960 by EMKA, Ltd. All rights reserved. Used with permission.

Love Happy, screenplay by Frank Tashlin and Mac Benoff, based on a story by Harpo Marx; Lester Cowan / Mary Pickford, 1949.

Monkey Business, screenplay by Arthur Sheekman, from a story by S. J. Perelman, Roland Pertwee, and W. B. Johnstone. Copyright © 1931 Paramount Publix Corp. Renewed 1958 by EMKA, Ltd. All rights reserved. Used with permission.

A Night at the Opera, screenplay by George S. Kaufman and Morrie Ryskind. Copyright © 1935 Warner Brothers Entertainment, Inc. All rights reserved. Used with permission.

A Night in Casablanca, original screenplay by Joseph Fields and Roland Kibbee. Copyright © 1946 Loma Vista Productions, Inc. Renewed © 1974 Gummo Marx. All rights reserved. Used with permission.

Room Service, screenplay by Morrie Ryskind, based on the play by John Murray and Allen Boretz. Copyright © 1938 RKO Pictures, Inc. All rights reserved. Used with permission.

Television Dialogue

You Bet Your Life. From *The Secret Word Is Groucho* by Groucho Marx with Hector Arce (New York: G. P. Putnam's Sons, 1976). Copyright © 1976 by Groucho Marx. All rights reserved. Reprinted with permission.

Stage Dialogue

Home Again, vaudeville act performed in 1914 and written by Al Sheen.

I'll Say She Is!, Broadway play, performed in 1924 and written by Will B. Johnstone and Groucho Marx.

Radio Dialogue

Beagle, Shyster, and Beagle, Episode 3, December 12, 1932 (on page 176).

Flywheel, Shyster, and Flywheel, Episode 23, May 1, 1933 (on pages 70 and 120).

Song Lyrics

"HOORAY FOR CAPTAIN SPAULDING" by Bert Kalmar and Harry Ruby. Copyright © 1936 (Renewed) Warner Bros. Inc. (ASCAP) and Memory Lane Music Ltd. (PRS). All Rights Reserved. Used by Permission. Warner Bros. Publications U.S. Inc., Miami, FL 33014.

"LYDIA, THE TATTOOED LADY," by E. Y. Harburg and Harold Arlen. Copyright © 1939 (Renewed) EMI Feist Catalog Inc. All rights reserved. Used by permission. Warner Bros. Publications U.S. Inc., Miami, FL 33014.

Books and Writings

As Long As They're Laughing: Groucho Marx and You Bet Your Life by Robert Dwan (Baltimore, Maryland: Midnight Marquee Press, 2000). Copyright © 2000 by Robert Dwan. All rights reserved. Reprinted with permission.

"Bad Days Are Good Memories" by Groucho Marx, *The Saturday Evening Post,* August 29, 1931. Copyright © 1931 Groucho Marx. All rights reserved. Reprinted with permission.

Beds by Groucho Marx (Indianapolis, Indiana: Bobbs-Merrill, 1976). Copyright © 1930 by Julius H. Marx, renewed 1976. All rights reserved. Reprinted with permission.

Groucho and Me by Groucho Marx (New York: Bernard Geis Associates, 1959). Copyright © 1959 by Groucho Marx. All rights reserved. Reprinted with permission.

"Groucho Blasts TV, the Critics, Comedians—Even Eisenhower" by Joe Hyams, *Boston Globe,* January 22, 1960, page 9.

The Groucho Letters: Letters From and To Groucho Marx by Groucho Marx (New York: Simon & Schuster, 1967). Copyright © 1967 by Groucho Marx, copyright renewed 1995 by Miriam Marx Allen, Arthur Marx, and Melinda Marx. All rights reserved. Reprinted with permission.

"Groucho Marx Turns Himself In For Scrap" by Groucho Marx, *New York Herald Tribune, This Week,* November 8, 1942. Copyright © 1942 by Groucho Marx. All rights reserved. Reprinted with permission.

The Groucho Phile: An Illustrated Life by Groucho Marx (Indianapolis: Bobbs-Merrill Company, Inc., 1976). Copyright © 1976 by Groucho Marx. All rights reserved. Reprinted with permission.

"How to Be a Spy" by Groucho Marx, *This Week,* February 16, 1946. Copyright © 1946 by Groucho Marx. All rights reserved. Reprinted with permission.

"How to Build a Secret Weapon" by Groucho Marx, *This Week,* November 7, 1943. Copyright © 1943 by Groucho Marx. All rights reserved. Reprinted with permission.

"King Leer" by Groucho Marx, *Tele-Views* (September 1950). Copyright © 1950 by Groucho Marx. All rights reserved. Reprinted with permission.

Love, Groucho: Letters from Groucho Marx to His Daughter Miriam by Groucho Marx, edited by Miriam Marx Allen (Boston: Faber and Faber, 1992). Copyright © 1992 by Miriam Marx Allen. All rights reserved. Reprinted with permission.

Many Happy Returns by Groucho Marx (New York: Simon & Schuster, 1942). Copyright © 1942 by Groucho Marx. All rights reserved. Reprinted with permission.

Memoirs of a Mangy Lover by Groucho Marx (New York: Bernard Geis Associates, 1963). Copyright © 1963 by Groucho Marx. All rights reserved. Reprinted with permission.

"My Best Friend Is a Dog . . ." by Groucho Marx (*This Week,* circa 1941), reprinted in *The Groucho Phile.* Copyright © 1976 by Groucho Marx. All rights reserved. Reprinted with permission.

My Life with Groucho by Arthur Marx (London: Robson, 1988). Copyright © 1988 by Arthur Marx. All rights reserved. Reprinted with permission.

The Secret Word Is Groucho by Groucho Marx with Hector Arce (New York: G. P. Putnam's Sons, 1976). Copyright © 1976 by Groucho Marx. All rights reserved. Reprinted with permission.

"That Marx Guy Again" by Groucho Marx, *Variety,* August 23, 1934. Copyright © 1934 by Groucho Marx. All rights reserved. Reprinted with permission.

Untitled Column by Groucho Marx, *Variety,* June 7, 1947. Copyright © 1947 by Groucho Marx. All rights reserved. Reprinted with permission.

"What This Country Needs" by Groucho Marx, *This Week,* June 16, 1940. Copyright © 1940 by Groucho Marx. All rights reserved. Reprinted with permission.

JOHN LENNON

Movie Dialogue

A Hard Day's Night, script by Alun Owen. Copyright © 1964 and 1995 by Walter Shenson Films. All rights reserved.

Let It Be, documentary directed by Michael Lindsay-Hogg. Copyright © 1970 by Apple Films. All rights reserved.

Books and Writings

"An Alphabet" by John Lennon. Copyright © 1969 by John Lennon, renewed 1986 by The Estate of John Lennon and Yoko Ono. All rights reserved. Used by permission.

"Being a Short Diversion on the Dubious Origins of Beatles" by John Lennon, *Mersey Beat,* July 6, 1961. Copyright © 1961 by John Lennon. All rights reserved. Used by permission.

Daily Howl by John Lennon (his writings in high school).

"Dear World Letter," 1970. Copyright © 1970 by John Lennon and Yoko Ono, renewed 2000 by Yoko Ono Lennon. All rights reserved. Reprinted with permission.

In His Own Write by John Lennon (New York: Simon & Schuster, 1964). Copyright © 1964, renewed 1992 by Yoko Ono. Used by permission. All rights reserved.

Interview by Larry Kane, September 13, 1964, reprinted from *Ticket to Ride* by Larry Kane (Philadelphia: Running Press, 2003). Copyright © 2003 by Larry Kane. All rights reserved. Used with permission.

"Jock and Yono" by John Lennon. Copyright © 1968 by John Lennon, renewed 1986 by The Estate of John Lennon and Yoko Ono. All rights reserved. Reprinted with permission.

Lennon Remembers: The Rolling Stone Interviews by Jann Wenner (New York: Popular Library, 1971). Copyright © 1971 by Straight Arrow Books. All rights reserved. Reprinted with permission.

Playboy Interview: The Beatles, *Playboy* magazine (February 1965). Copyright © 1965 by Playboy. All rights reserved. Reprinted with permission.

Playboy Interview: John Lennon and Yoko Ono, *Playboy* magazine (January 1981). Copyright © 1980 by Playboy. All rights reserved. Reprinted with permission.

Quote from Nat Weiss, *The Ballad of John and Yoko* by the editors of *Rolling Stone,* edited by Jonathan Cott and Christine Doudna (New York: Doubleday, 1982). Copyright © 1982 by Rolling Stone Press. All rights reserved. Reprinted with permission.

Song Lyrics: Lennon/McCartney

Music Square West, Nashville, TN 37203. All rights reserved. Used by permission.

"THE WORD" by John Lennon and Paul McCartney. Copyright © 1965 Sony/ATV (Renewed) Sony/ATV Tunes LLC. All rights administered by Sony/ATV Music Publishing, 8 Music Square West, Nashville, TN 37203. All rights reserved. Used by permission.

"YOU WON'T SEE ME" by John Lennon and Paul McCartney. Copyright © 1965 Sony/ATV (Renewed) Sony/ATV Tunes LLC. All rights administered by Sony/ATV Music Publishing, 8 Music Square West, Nashville, TN 37203. All rights reserved. Used by permission.

Song Lyrics: Lennon/Ono

"FORTUNATELY" by John Lennon and Yoko Ono. Vignette from "Bed-In," 1969. © 1998 Yoko Ono. All Rights for the U.S. and Canada Controlled and Administered by *SBK Blackwood Music Inc.* All Rights Reserved. International Copyright Secured. Used by Permission.

"LUCK OF THE IRISH" by John Lennon and Yoko Ono. © 1972 *Lenono Music/Ono Music.* All Rights for the U.S. and Canada Controlled and Administered by *SBK Blackwood Music Inc.* All Rights Reserved. International Copyright Secured. Used by Permission.

"OH MY LOVE" by John Lennon and Yoko Ono. © 1973 *Lenono Music/Ono Music.* All Rights for the U.S. and Canada Controlled and Administered by *SBK Blackwood Music Inc.* All Rights Reserved. International Copyright Secured. Used by Permission.

"WOMAN IS THE NIGGER OF THE WORLD" by John Lennon and Yoko Ono. © 1972 *Lenono Music/Ono Music.* All Rights for the U.S. and Canada Controlled and Administered by *SBK Blackwood Music Inc.* All Rights Reserved. International Copyright Secured. Used by Permission.

Song Lyrics: John Lennon

"BEAUTIFUL BOY (DARLING BOY)" by John Lennon. © 1980 *Lenono Music.* All Rights for the U.S. and Canada Controlled and Administered by *SBK Blackwood Music Inc.* All Rights Reserved. International Copyright Secured. Used by Permission.

Index of Quotes

About the Author

JOEY GREEN, the author of more than thirty books, including *Jesus and Muhammad: The Parallel Sayings*, *The Zen of Oz*, and *The Road to Success Is Paved with Failure*, has appeared on *The Tonight Show with Jay Leno*, *The Rosie O'Donnell Show*, *Today*, *The View*, *Late Night with Conan O'Brien*, *Dateline NBC*, and *Good Morning, America*. He has been profiled in the *New York Times*, *People*, *Entertainment Weekly*, and the *Los Angeles Times*. A former contributing editor to *National Lampoon* and a former advertising copywriter at J. Walter Thompson, Green is a graduate of Cornell University, backpacked around the world for two years on his honeymoon, and lives in Los Angeles with his wife, Debbie, and their two daughters, Ashley and Julia.

YOKO ONO, the author of *Grapefruit*, has created revolutionary forms of music, film, and the visual arts since the 1960s, when she emerged as an avant-garde force in New York, Tokyo, and London. She was married to John Lennon from 1969 until his death in 1980. Together, the two formed the Plastic Ono Band and spent much of their time on peace and humanitarian efforts. Ono continues her artistic endeavors as a writer, painter, and musician. She lives in New York City.

ARTHUR MARX, the son of Groucho Marx, has written radio scripts for Milton Berle, several films for Bob Hope, and television episodes for Lucille Ball. He co-authored several Broadway hits with Robert Fischer, including *The Impossible Years* starring Alan King, *Minnie's Boys* starring Shelley Winters, and *Groucho: A Life in Revue*, starring Frank Ferrante. He has written a dozen books, including *My Life With Groucho*, *The Secret Life of Bob Hope*, *Goldwyn*, and *The Nine Lives of Mickey Rooney*. A contributor to the *New York Times Magazine*, *Sports Illustrated*, *Parade*, and *Cigar Aficionado*, Marx lives in Los Angeles.

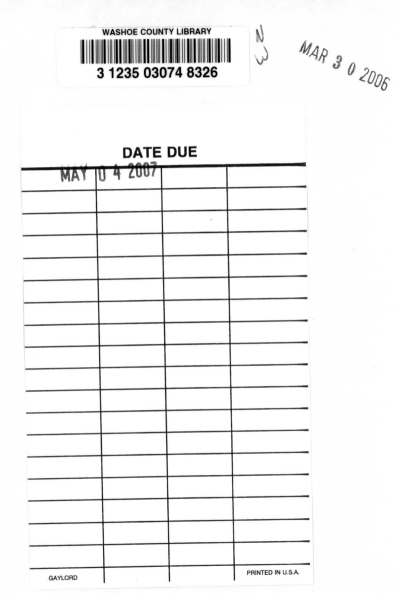